Male Victims of Same-Sex Abuse

Male Victims of Same-Sex Abuse
Addressing Their Sexual Response

John M. Preble
and A. Nicholas Groth

Sidran Press
Baltimore, Maryland

Printed in the United States of America

ISBN 1-886968-13-6

The Adult Male Sexual Victimization Questionnaire (appendix) is reproduced courtesy of Forensic Mental Health Associates, © 1980.

Cover illustration and text ornament: detail from Perham W. Nahl's "Thirteenth Labor of Hercules," Panama Pacific International Exposition, San Francisco, 1915

DEDICATION

In loving memory of my mother
SOPHIE MARY (KARABASH) GROTH
1904–1991
A. N. G.

For their love and support, I dedicate this
book to my wife, Celeste; my son, Jacob; my
daughter, Lauren; my mother, Jeanne Preble;
and in memory of my father, Kenneth J. Preble

J. M. P.

Contents

Foreword

This book will be helpful to every clinician who works with male victims of sexual assault. Indeed, it will be helpful to all clinicians who work with male clients in any type of therapeutic setting (whether or not sexual victimization is the focus of the therapy). A. Nicholas Groth and John Preble are clinicians who have an aggregate of 40 years of clinical experience in working with male victims and perpetrators of sexual assault in both community and institutional settings. In this manual, they offer a straightforward and reassuring framework that is pertinent for all therapists for understanding male sexuality and the dynamics of sexual assault.

Why is this book so important? Unfortunately, useful information on these subjects still is not being presented by most university training programs for clinicians. And even now, few workshops or staff development programs offer practical information on working with issues of male sexuality or sexual assault of males. In particular, little has been published about the sexual dynamics of male sexual victimization.

Amazingly, the sexual aspects of sexual abuse have been downplayed in the past two decades. Emphasis has been placed instead on the dynamics of aggression in sexual abuse (in order to combat public misunderstanding about this behavior). John Preble and Nick Groth now are restoring the missing dynamic by "putting the sex back into sexual assault" in this manual. Their text offers the clinician a systematic way of addressing the sexual dynamics of sexual assault with male clients. Practical guidelines (including samples of what to say to clients) are provided for helping male victims understand and come to terms with what occurred during and after the sexual assault. Since so many instances of male sexual victimization go unreported and unaddressed, this book should be required reading for all clinicians.

> Suzanne M. Sgroi, M.D.
> Director, New England
> Clinical Associates
> West Hartford, CT

Suzanne M. Sgroi, M.D., is the author of the *Handbook of Clinical Intervention in Child Sexual Abuse* (Lexington Books, 1982), *Vulnerable Populations*, Vols. 1 & 2 (Lexington Books, 1989), and, along with Ann W. Burgess, A. Nicholas Groth, and Lynda Lytle Holmstrom, of *Sexual Assault of Children and Adolescents* (Lexington Books, 1978).

Acknowledgments

We wish to express our appreciation to a number of people who have contributed to our understanding of this serious social issue and to the many individuals who have been of support and assistance to us both professionally and personally throughout the course of our professional lives. We are indebted to the many offenders and victims of sexual assault whom we have come to know in the course of our professional work. By sharing their experiences, some of which we have quoted in this text, they have helped to advance our knowledge and understanding of this subject.

We especially would like to acknowledge three giants in the field who we can proudly claim as friends as well as colleagues: Suzanne M. Sgroi, M.D., Director of New England Clinical Associates in West Hartford, Connecticut; Ann Wolbert Burgess, D.N.Sc., Professor of Psychiatric Nursing at Boston College, Chestnut Hill, Massachusetts; and Fred S. Berlin, M.D., Ph.D., Director of the National Institute for the Study, Treatment, and Prevention of Sexual Trauma in Baltimore, Maryland.

Acknowledgments

Thanks, too, to H. Jean Birnbaum, Linda Blick, Jan M. Delipsey, Stella Gallegos, and Lois A. Norling for their encouragement and unwavering support and assistance. In this work, as in life, it is essential to have a good support system and no one could ask for better friends than these five special women.

We are grateful to Maria Iantosca for typing and editing the initial draft of our manuscript, to Mary Lou Kenney for her editing of this work, and especially to Linda Blick and Esther Giller for making this publication possible.

A. Nicholas Groth
Orlando, Florida

In addition, I want to express my sincere appreciation to Nick Groth who has been and will continue to be an excellent teacher, a true mentor, and a valued friend. Thank you, Nick.

John M. Preble
Temecula, California

Introduction

This text is not an overall, inclusive approach to working with male victims of sexual abuse. There are a number of excellent books currently available that address this topic and we have listed them under Recommended Readings. Although these texts offer a generic approach to the task of recovering from being sexually victimized, helping the male victim process the sexual aspects or dimensions of his experience remains, for the most part, unaddressed. This, then, is the focus of our text which will serve as a supplement and complement to the available literature. It is designed to help the client specifically understand his sexual reactions or responses during such victimization. Therefore, this is not written from a perspective of *investigating* sexual abuse, but as a guide for clinical work.

Further, this text addresses mature sexual experience and behavior and is directed, for the most part, toward the older adolescent and adult male victim of sexual abuse. Although some of this material may be used with younger male victims, it needs to be done judiciously, since prepubertal males do not have a conceptual or experiential understanding of mature sexual processes and functioning. We have offered some nonsexual analogies aimed at the sexually immature and inexperienced youngster to address similar issues, but the primary emphasis in this text is directed toward sexually mature males for whom the victimization has involved sexual responses and reactions.

At the conclusion of the text we have appended a questionnaire which was originally designed as an instrument for data collection and study, but which has proven useful as an outline and a guide for the clinician to explore in a systematic fashion with the client the various aspects and dimensions of the sexual activity involved in the event. It is specifically designed for sexually mature males. It is not appropriate to use with children. We have found that some males are more comfortable filling out this questionnaire privately at the start rather than verbally narrating the nature of their sexual victimization. However, this questionnaire does not stand alone. It is an aid to exploring the dimensions of the sexual victimization; it is not a substitute for clinical work in this regard. However, it can assist the client and the clinician in helping to focus on and understand the dynamics of the sexual victimization.

Human Sexuality and Victimization

Sexual victimization involves the abuse of power. Knowledge is power. An understanding of the nature of human sexuality is needed in order to provide a means for the male victim of sexual abuse to process his experience and address his victimization. Why is male sexual victimization often overlooked? What can it mean to a male to be victimized sexually? What is the difference between being victimized and being traumatized? What are the different aspects of a male's sexual make-up? What is the victim's understanding of male sexuality and his own sexual nature? What are his attitudes about this? The chapters that follow address these questions and provide a conceptual framework or guide for understanding human sexuality. One of the first steps then in helping a victim become empowered involves sex education—or reeducation.

Chapter One

The Elements of Victimization

Since the advent of the child protection movement in the 1970s, we have become increasingly aware of the prevalence of child sexual abuse in our society. In the majority of reported cases, the victim is a female child. It is thought, however, that boys may be as much at risk of being molested as are girls, but that the sexual abuse of males is underreported for a variety of reasons.

Factors Discouraging Disclosure

Attention to sexual assault has resulted from the emergence of the rape crisis movement, which addressed the needs of women victims, and from the child protection movement, which placed primary emphasis on intrafamilial sexual abuse, a context in which girls appear to be at greater risk than boys. Consequently, the male victim of sexual assault has received less public attention than the female victim, and the average person appears less alert to the risk of boys and men being sexually victimized.

In the development of males in our society, role expectations place a premium on self-sufficiency and independence. Males are not expected to be vulnerable. In the face of adversity they are expected to "fight their own battles" and not turn to others for help or assistance. Therefore, if a boy is taken advantage of sexually, he may perceive this as evidence of failure on his part to be invincible, and that to report this would expose his personal defect to others. To turn to others for help would only further testify to his inability to take care of himself and take charge of his life. Attributing such psychological meaning to the event would inhibit him from reporting himself to be a victim.

Also in their socialization as males, boys learn they are expected to be strong and tough: *"Big boys don't cry."* Vulnerability is regarded as weakness and emotions such as fear and sadness are regarded as unmanly. Therefore, when adversity strikes, males are not expected to complain: *"brush it off,"* *"tough it out,"* *"don't let it bother you."* To acknowledge the experience of being victimized is to subject oneself to feelings of humiliation, defeat, and failure in regard to the tests of manhood. For males the message often is: *"don't get sad, get mad—or better still—get even!"* He should not acknowledge emotional pain. Disturbing thoughts or feelings should be suppressed or forgotten, not acknowledged or discussed.

A male's sexuality is a major test of his manhood. A "real" man is generally regarded as someone who is unequivocally straight (heterosexual) in his desires and activities. When a male is sexually victimized by another male, this is literally (although in most cases not psychologically) a homosexual event, and the victim's manhood has been tampered with and compromised. He feels his sexuality has been tainted and he has been disgraced as a male. Fear of such stigmatization may lead the male victim to suppress disclosure in order to conceal the event from his parents or others whose opinions matter to him.

> *After I was molested I used to be concerned a lot about whether I looked effeminate. I remember that I didn't like my body because I thought I was too thin. All the guys I looked up to were somewhat muscular and tough. I thought the guy who molested me picked me because I looked vulnerable. Anyway, I started working out with weights and I studied martial arts for a while. I felt like he stole my manhood and I was going to get it back.*

If, on the other hand, the boy is taken advantage of sexually by a female, this is often not regarded as victimization. Rather than viewing this as tampering with his masculinity, our culture sees this as an introduction to his manhood, and the boy is ridiculed for complaining. This is an experience to be welcomed and enjoyed. He is not allowed to be frightened or confused or to feel inadequate or taken advantage of—this is his sex education. He's a lucky guy, a real "stud." Any other feelings may raise doubts about his manhood.

> *I was molested by this older boy in my neighborhood when I was in first grade. He was a couple years older than me. He did oral sex on me a couple times. I worried later that I would become a homosexual. An older girl also molested me when I was in the fifth grade. I think she was in high school because she was a lot older than me. This girl lived down the street and apparently had shown my buddy her breasts and he got a big kick out of it. She took us into her room and she whipped off her top, we whipped out our penises and said, "Boy this*

is great stuff!" She didn't touch us or anything the first time. We just showed her what she'd accomplished (erections) and she seemed to get a charge out of it. Then at a later date all three of us went over to a park. We went into the men's bathroom. Standing up she dropped her trousers and told me to drop mine, then maneuvered my penis around until I guess it was in her pussy. I don't know for sure, I don't remember it feeling warm. I guess it was, but I didn't know anything about pelvic motion or anything. I just stood there and she counted to a certain number and said, "Okay that's it." I remember my thought being, "Is that all it is? There's nothing so great about sex." I never really thought it would bother me. In fact I never told anyone about the guy that molested me but I did tell a few of my friends about the girl. That one I wasn't ashamed of. It was with a girl so I thought at least it was all right. You know it's natural like it says in the Bible that a man goes with a woman. The funny thing is nobody believed me about the girl, that I had sex in the fifth grade. It was like "Wow! No way, nobody's lucky enough to get laid in the fifth grade!" I would say "Yeah, this chick liked young guys; she was showing me the ropes," or something like that. It was like all these movies that come out with the older woman and the younger boy. Now I feel differently about it. I think I got laid at too young an age. I really didn't enjoy it. She was in total control.

Boys may be allowed more unsupervised activities than girls of the same age, and if in this context he is sexually victimized, a boy may be reluctant to report the event as this may result in a loss of his freedom and independence. His parents or caretakers may increase their supervision of him or curtail his unsupervised activities or play.

Encouraged to be more adventuresome than girls, boys may be more easily entrapped in sexual exploitation in the context of some other forbidden activity, such as looking at pornographic magazines, smoking (marijuana) or drinking, participating in petty shoplifting, etc. He then is deterred from reporting the sexual abuse due to the fear of others discovering his involvement in the prohibited activity.

Social values and male role expectations may also serve to mask indications of sexual victimization in male behavior. For example, a girl who is sexually abused might reflect this during adolescence through compulsive, indiscriminate sexual activity with boys. Usually note is taken of such behavior and this girl acquires a reputation of being "easy" or promiscuous. Her behavior is seen, in some respects, as inappropriate.

However, if a boy who has been sexually abused displays similar compulsive and indiscriminate sexual behavior with girls as he enters adolescence, it is not viewed as equally inappropriate. Instead it may be regarded as typical male adolescent sexual behavior to be expected—*"he's just sowing his wild oats."* No special note is taken. The idea of this behavior indicating prior sexual victimization does not occur to others. Even sexually assaultive behavior on the part of juvenile males is often misidentified as normative adolescent sexual activity. In some cases, increased aggression is an aftermath of sexual victimization, but this behavior too may be simply regarded as characteristic of male development during adolescence. Hence boys are less likely to be identified as victims of sexual abuse than are girls in cases of undisclosed victimization.

The concept of victimization is also one that males have more difficulty with in respect to self-identification. If the experience was sexually pleasurable, if they benefited from the involvement in some ways, if they got something they wanted in exchange, they are not as likely to feel they have been taken advantage of. They may regard their cooperation as collaboration and not feel transgressed against. Often they regard the sexual activity as *"something we did together"* rather than *"something [the offender] did to me."* They may not conceptualize their sexual victimization as abuse or assault. Asking a male if he has ever been a victim of sexual abuse without operationally defining the term may elicit a negative response even when such an event has in fact occurred in his life.

Victimization versus Traumatization

As clinicians we need to differentiate between a client's being *victimized* and his being **traumatized**. Sexual victimization refers to a situation in which an individual is taken advantage of or exploited in a sexual fashion. Traumatization refers to a situation in which such victimization damages or interferes with the individual's subsequent psychosocial adjustment or development. A person may be sexually victimized through enticement, manipulation, entrapment, extortion, intimidation, or force. Whether or not such an experience proves traumatic may depend on a number of factors such as

- the nature, frequency, or intensity of the event;
- the developmental stage of the victim, his preexisting coping skills, psychological resources, and genetic predispositions; and
- the availability and quality of his social support system—the reactions of significant other persons in his life to the disclosure or discovery of this event.

In working with such a client then, it may be helpful to differentiate:

- problems that were preexisting in his life (which would have been there even if he had not been sexually victimized);

- problems that preexisted in his life but were aggravated or intensified by his sexual victimization;
- problems that derive specifically from the sexual victimization experience; and
- problems that resulted from the revelation to others (disclosure or discovery) of his victimization.

Obviously these are not mutually exclusive and one may complicate another. Nor can the client perfectly separate them. But insofar as the client can attempt to differentiate among them and then assign some priority to the concerns this may facilitate his proceeding to address and resolve these issues in an organized and systematic fashion. It may help to say *"of all the various aspects of this event that we have talked about, what is the most troublesome to you?"* By breaking things down you can make a confusing and complex experience more approachable and manageable.

Sexual victimization, by definition, involves elements of both sexuality and aggression in an interpersonal context. For most males, sexuality is intrinsic to their sense of masculine identity and competency. Their sexual experiences are often regarded as a measure of their manhood and masculinity. For this reason, the primary emphasis in this text will be the common sexual concerns males experience when they have been sexually victimized by other males.

Chapter Two

Understanding Human Sexuality

Understanding One's Sexual Nature

As human beings we differ from one another in many ways in regard to our physical make-up. For example, we are not all the same height; some of us are tall, some of us are short, and most of us are of average height. We have different skin tones, body shapes, and hair colors. In fact, it is the rare exception when two or more people have an identical appearance. Human beings are different in regard to the nature of their sexuality, too, and this can be categorized in five basic ways: the objects of their erotic interests; the nature of their sexual activities; the intensity of their sexual desires; attitudes toward their own sexuality; and their self-control.

Objects of Erotic Interest

One way in which people differ from each other sexually is in regard to the types of persons they find appealing as sexual partners. Not everyone finds the same kind of individual sexually attractive. Although it appears that most people are attracted to persons of the opposite sex, some people are attracted to persons of the same sex, and others find both males and females sexually appealing. Although most people appear to be sexually attracted to persons within their own generation, some persons are sexually drawn to young persons while others are attracted to persons much older than themselves. It might even be particular parts of the body that determines who an individual finds sexually appealing. One man might be aroused by the size of a woman's breasts or the shape of her legs, whereas another might be "turned on" by the shape of a man's buttocks or the size of his biceps. In fact, a person usually finds that it is the combination of a number of physical characteristics that elicits sexual interest on his part in another person. In any case, one of the basic ways in which people differ from each other sexually is in regard to the types of partners they experience as sexually desirable.

The Nature of Sexual Activities

Another way in which people differ from each other is in regard to the types of sexual acts they find pleasurable, enjoyable, and erotically exciting. We don't all find the same things sexually pleasurable. Some persons enjoy kissing and cuddling a great deal and other people do not. For some people masturbation is the favorite sexual activity, whereas for others intercourse is. Some people enjoy oral sex; some people do not. Most people find that a variety of sexual acts are, to different degrees, pleasurable, but some people may experience certain behaviors as sexually exciting that most people do not experience in that fashion. For example, some people may find that sexually exposing themselves is erotically exciting to them, or that they enjoy being spanked when having sex, or that they become aroused by cross-dressing. People differ from each other then in regard to the types of sexual behaviors they find enjoyable and in the kinds of activities that enhance the erotic pleasure they experience in such acts.

Intensity of Sexual Desires

The third basic way in which people differ in regard to their sexual natures is the frequency and intensity of their sexual desire. Some people have very strong sexual appetites, whereas others seem to have less intense desires. For example, some people desire sex every day or even several times a day; others engage in sex only on occasion and others, seldom if at all. Some people describe compelling sexual urges that take on the quality of an addiction or irresistible impulse. Others seem less driven by sexual needs. Not only does the intensity of sexual desires differ among people but such sexual energy may differ within the same individual at different times in life, influenced by such factors as age, physical health, mood state, and the like.

Attitude toward One's Own Sexuality

Human beings differ then in regard to their sexuality just as they differ in regard to other physical traits. Probably no two people have an identical sexual nature, and although many people will display similar characteristics in regard to their patterns of sexual arousal or interest, each person has some unique features as well. People differ among themselves in respect to whom they find sexually appealing, what they find sexually satisfying, and when they feel like engaging in sexual behavior. Some people have ordinary sexual interests, whereas other people have unusual sexual interests. People are different. Just as some people are right-handed, others left-handed, and some ambidextrous, so, too, some people are heterosexually oriented, others are homosexually oriented, and some are bisexually oriented.

In our society, however, some traits are advantages and other traits are disadvantages in regard to social norms. For example, although there is nothing intrinsically good or bad in regard to the color of one's skin, it is more advantageous to be white in our society than to be black—one is less likely to be discriminated against. And although we may accept the fact that people differ in regard to height and recognize there is nothing wrong in being short, it is regarded as more desirable for a man to be tall. However, due to the fact that we live in a sexually uneducated and sexually prejudiced society, when it comes to a person's sexual nature, any departure from conventional sexual orientation or traditional sexual behavior is often equated with pathology and met with strong social disapproval. To discover one is different from most people in regard to one's sexuality is an unsettling event. Rather than understanding that the nature of human sexuality encompasses wide diversity and variety, a person making such a discovery often regards it as a secret shame that intrinsically diminishes his or her worth as a person.

As a result, people differ from each other in a fourth way: in regard to their attitudes toward their own sexual desires and experiences. Insofar as an individual's desires differ from conventional sexual interests he or she has to come to terms with this fact of life in some fashion. Unfortunately most people do not have the opportunity to sort out the nature of their sexuality or to clarify their values in this regard. As a result, due to an unintended sexual experience, they may suffer considerable distress or anxiety over the personal implications of such an event; or, discovering that they have unconventional sexual interests, experience anguish and desperation in regard to such unwanted desires.

Self-Control

It is also important to appreciate that individuals differ in regard to their ability to *resist* unwanted sexual desires. For some persons such desires may be experienced as irresistible urges or compulsions.

> *My introduction to sex came from my half-brother. My father had two sons from his first marriage. I was somewhere between six and eight years old and my half-brother was about five years older than me. When they would visit he and I would sleep together on the sofa bed. One night he performed oral sex on me. It felt great, but he wanted me to suck him also. At first I did not want to, but if I didn't suck him, he wouldn't suck me, so I did. I was confused about this. It felt good and I enjoyed it, but it had to be a secret or we would get into trouble. This happened off and on for a few years. Sometime after this I decided to show some of my friends what I had learned. I can remember several instances in which I was the instigator of oral sex with them. We never came off—I think we were too young for that. It just felt good. I can remember being confused about my sexuality, thinking that I might be a homosexual. My stepfather was into reading* Playboy *and I found out where he kept them in his closet. Every night when I would take my shower I would sneak into his closet and grab some magazines and would masturbate, looking at them. By this time I was coming off. I would*

often masturbate once or twice a day if not more. This was very confusing to me. I am married now and I'm still confused about my sexuality. I tend to think I'm a sexaholic. I do not seem to be able to control my sexual thoughts. Everything is sexual to me.

Even though a person may regard his sexual desires or urges as unacceptable or unwanted, this alone does not necessarily mean he has the ability to refrain from such behavior. If simply *regarding* a behavior as unhealthy or inappropriate or even harmful were sufficient, no one would, for example, eat or drink too much. What we are referring to here is the concept of *self-control*—not whether a person refrains from unwanted behavior in the presence of external authority or control, but whether he is able to do so when there is nothing to stop him except his own ability or will power. Individuals differ in their ability to inhibit unwanted sexual urges or to resist unwanted sexual temptations. Whereas *intensity* of sexual feelings (see page 12) refers to the strength of desire, in this section we are emphasizing the strength of a person's *control* over desire and the many psychological and/or situational factors—the inhibitors and disinhibitors—that may affect this at different times.

Misconceptions about Sexuality

Because in most cases of sexual victimization of males both the victim and perpetrator are males, one of the predominant issues in regard to impact and recovery is the homosexual character of this event. How can we aid the male victim in this regard? What is useful in helping him understand the nature of this experience in his life?

First of all, things must be looked at in perspective. Many of the prevailing attitudes toward sexuality—both traditional

15

and unconventional—are not based on scientific study or fact but instead have their roots in historical, religious, legal, or philosophical ideas that predate psychology (the study of human behavior) or sexology (the scientific study of sexual behavior). As advances are made in understanding human behavior, attitudes need to be amended in light of expanding knowledge and information.

For example, around the turn of the twentieth century the prevailing medical opinion in regard to masturbation was that it was a "vice." It constituted "self-abuse," which had pathological consequences mentally, emotionally, and physically and was to be guarded against as unnatural and unhealthy. We can imagine the needless distress and suffering that resulted when a youngster could not resist the temptation of self-gratification and, according to expert medical opinion, thus risked impotency, sterility, blindness, moral dissipation, and even insanity.

Today we are able to recognize the nonsense of such attitudes and beliefs toward masturbation and even joke about the absurd idea of "going blind." Yet, as recently as 1990 the Surgeon General of the United States was forced to resign as a result of the controversy surrounding her advocacy of masturbation as a safe alternative to teenage sexual intercourse. A subsequent Surgeon General experienced criticism for his advocacy of establishing responsible sex education starting in early childhood. Unfortunately, in a society that does not educate its youth in regard to sexuality, old misconceptions are often replaced by new misconceptions. In our work with adolescent males, for example, we frequently encounter denial in regard to masturbation and the belief that such activity would mean they are homosexual.

What can we say truthfully about the nature of human sexuality in regard to its manifest diversity and variety? Perhaps we can approach this by first identifying two basic and related points that are not sufficiently appreciated in regard to understanding human sexuality: *discovery versus choice* and *character versus sexuality.*

Discovering versus Choosing

First, no matter how sexual interests are formed, we do not voluntarily **choose** the nature of our sexuality—we **discover** it. As we sexually mature we find out what stimulates us sexually and what types of sexual activities are pleasurable. If you are a man who finds women sexually appealing, you did not decide as a youngster to have such heterosexual interests; you discovered such inclinations as you entered puberty—or even before—and matured sexually. Similarly if you are a male who finds other males sexually appealing, you discovered this about your sexual nature; you did not decide that this would be the nature of your sexuality. No one chooses his sexuality any more than he chooses his height, skin tone, the color of his eyes, or his original language. No male *decides* what will elicit an erection on his part; rather, he *discovers* what will sexually arouse him. He discovers as he enters adolescence, or even before, what is sexually tempting or erotic to him.

However sexual interests are created, they are not willed into being. Most likely, sexuality, like other human traits, is the result of both nature and nurture in varying combinations. Many variables play a role in forming one's sexuality: biological inheritance or genetics; constitutional factors; the events that transpire during one's developmental years; the social context of these events; and the upbringing and behavior models one has. How these contributing factors are weighted and combined will vary from person to person, and people might arrive at similar sexual destinations by extremely different routes. We do not know all the factors that need to occur, in what combinations, at what critical points in development, in what relationships to each other, with what intensities, and in what contexts for a person to arrive at his particular sexual nature. But we do know that none of these factors is under his control. He is not able to select or eradicate such influences. He is only able to discover the nature of the final product, the nature of his sexuality. How he conducts himself, whether or not he pursues his sexual inclinations, and, if so, in what manner, is where choice comes into the picture—but what he *finds* tempting sexually is not due to volitional choice. If his sexual inclinations or orientation are such as is traditional in our society, he should consider himself most fortunate. It behooves such a person to have compassion toward those for whom life has not been so kind sexually.

Character versus Sexuality

The second critical point in understanding human sexuality is that the nature of one's **sexual desires** and **interests** is separate and distinct from the nature of one's **character** or **personality**. Knowing the nature of a person's sexuality does not in and of itself reveal the nature of his character. For example, to know that Mr. Straight is an adult male who is heterosexually oriented, married, and who engages weekly in intercourse with his wife does not tell us *anything* about his character. Is Mr. Straight an honest or dishonest man? Is he kind or cruel? Loyal or unfaithful? Generous or selfish? Responsible or irresponsible? Bright or dull? Friendly or unfriendly? Criminal or law-abiding? Industrious or lazy? Mature or immature? We don't know. Personality traits and character traits are separate and distinct from sexuality or sexual orientation.

However, people often confuse sexuality with character and erroneously assume that a person with an unconventional sexual orientation will also be different in other respects from someone who has a more traditional sexual orientation. This is just not so. There are, for example, as many individual differences among men who are sexually attracted to other males as there are among men who are not sexually attracted to other males. The only difference between these two groups of men is that the former finds males sexually appealing and the latter does not. The sexuality of a person does not reveal his character any more than the character of a person reveals his sexuality. The worth of a man should not be measured by whom he goes to bed with, and those who judge themselves or others in this fashion do a serious injustice. It is not whom you go to bed with, but how you treat the person you go to bed with that reveals what kind of person you are.

Unfortunately we live in a society that is largely sexually ignorant. Ignorance leads to fear, and fear leads to anger, and neither frame of mind is conducive to clear thinking and rational judgment. The homophobic nature of our society indicates that considerable misunderstanding or ignorance prevails with respect to sexual activity between persons of the same sex. Not understanding conventional sexuality very clearly, people are even more confused and alarmed about nontraditional sexual behavior. It is not surprising then that myths and misconceptions regarding homosexuality abound in a society that does not endorse same-sex sexual behavior.

When we blur the boundaries between consensual homosexuality and same-sex abuse it serves to complicate and aggravate the impact of the victimization experience.

Sexual Values of the Clinician

To address the impact of sexual victimization on a male and facilitate his recovery often requires reeducation in regard to the nature of human sexuality. Few persons receive dependable information in regard to sexuality that prepares them for this aspect of their development. For some, sexual victimization is their introduction to sexuality, instilling a distorted perception. For others, it may be an event that is in confusing contrast to what they understood about the nature of sexuality. In order to be helpful to such clients it is important the intervener be clear in regard to his or her own understanding of human sexuality and recognize how attitudes and values may affect one's work.

For example, whether you hold pro-choice or anti-abortion views may affect how you work with a young girl who has been impregnated by her father. Similarly, whether you are strongly opposed to homosexuality or are gay-affirmative may influence the way you work with a male victim who was sexually abused by another male.

Although none of us is completely free from the norms and values of our society in regard to sexuality, it is important for us to explore and question these to guard against being biased or prejudiced in some respect. If you are going to do this work you need to be informed in regard to the nature of human sexuality and reasonably comfortable with addressing sexual material. You need to establish your own values in regard to the spectrum and diversity of human sexuality: what you find acceptable or unacceptable, what you find repulsive or threatening. And you then need to determine whether any negative values or feelings compromise your ability to respond to clients in such situations in a helpful or therapeutic fashion. Can you respect the fact that other persons may have different sexual values or attitudes? Can you recognize their right to pursue their own sexual happiness?

Does this mean that "anything goes"? If not, where do we draw the line? Our feeling is that anything goes as long as it 1) is consenting,* 2) poses no risk of direct harm to oneself or anyone else, and 3) does not restrict others who share different sexual interests from pursuing them.

It is the view of the authors that sexuality is, in itself, neither good nor bad but simply a behavior, like walking or eating or sleeping. Some sexual activities may pose a hazard to one's health and other sexual activities may pose a risk of harm to others. Where particular sexual acts are harmful, it is important to identify the risk and the evidence to support this. Sex is also a means of communication and can be evaluated in regard to its intent; for example, sometimes it is intended to be malicious or hostile. Basically, however, our view is that if it is consenting *adult* sexual activity, it is normal and acceptable, and if it is nonconsenting, it is criminal and pathological.

Note: Cooperation is **not** consent. For a sexual interaction to be consenting it requires the complete realization of what is transpiring and an understanding of the ramifications it has for the participants. It requires that the people involved have the physical and psychological freedom and competency to accept or refuse participation. For this reason sexual consent cannot ever exist between an adult and a child.

The Nature and Circumstances of Victimization

In order to help the victim of sexual abuse process his experience you should retrieve as much information as possible about the nature and circumstances of the victimization. How did the offender gain access to the victim? How old were the individuals involved? What type of sexual activity took place? What emotional reactions or responses accompanied the sexual victimization? What was the relationship between the offender and the victim? How often did the sexual abuse occur? How did the victimization get revealed? When other sources of information are available (such as police investigation reports, child protection assessments, witness accounts, medical examination records, offender statements, and the like) it is helpful to review them prior to interviewing the victim.

A questionnaire outlining the major aspects of the sexual victimization is provided as an appendix to this text. It serves as an interviewing guide for the clinician, but may also be an appropriate aid when the client finds discussing his sexual victimization acutely embarrassing. Having him fill out the questionnaire and then going over his written responses with him may serve to make addressing the event less difficult.

The chapters that follow amplify the key ideas outlined in the appendix. We discuss the strategies used by offenders, the types of relationships that exist between offender and victim, the nature of the sexual activity itself, the frequency of the victimization, and the manner in which the victimization came to light.

Chapter Three

Offender Strategies

There are a number of engagement strategies offenders use to involve victims in sexual activities. Through techniques of deception, enticement, manipulation, or entrapment, the perpetrator may *persuade* the victim to participate in the sexual activity. Or through threat, intimidation, force, or the misuse of authority he may *coerce* the victim to submit to or perform some unwanted sexual act. The type of strategy used to take advantage of a male sexually usually reflects the motivation of the perpetrator, but it can affect how the victim experiences the victimization. Let's take a closer look then at the ways in which an offender may access his victim sexually.

Persuasion Techniques

Persuasion techniques involve coaxing the victim in some fashion into the sexual activity.

Deception

The offender achieves sexual contact with the victim through some deceit or trick. He disguises the actual nature of the sexual abuse in some fashion or falsifies the true nature of what is actually occurring. For example, he may undress a child who has fallen down, explaining to the boy that he has to carefully examine him to see that he is not injured. Or a coach may tell a teenager on the swimming team that he must masturbate while his blood pressure is being taken as part of his physical exam. In such cases where deception occurs, the victim may not realize or appreciate at the time that he is being taken advantage of sexually, and later may feel dumb to have been so tricked.

Enticement

The offender tempts or bribes the victim into sexual activity by offering some incentive for his participation or reward for his cooperation. For example, he may tempt the boy with an offer of money in exchange for sexual favors or let a teenager use his car or motorcycle. In such cases where enticement is the strategy used, the victim receives something he wants in exchange for the sexual activity, so he may not feel he has been taken advantage of. He may not feel victimized since he agreed to the sexual contact or allowed it to occur.

Manipulation

The offender may subtly control and lead the victim into the sexual activity by endorsing or validating such behavior. For example, he may arouse a teenage boy's sexual interest by showing him some "adult" magazines and then talk the boy into being masturbated by saying, *"It's okay between friends— other guys do this too."* Or the offender may make his victim feel obligated or indebted to him in some fashion and then solicit sex as a means of repayment: *"I've been real good to you; I've done a lot of things to make you happy. Well now you can do something that would make me happy—something to show you appreciate everything I've done for you."* In other instances the offender may use his own child or an engaged victim as a decoy to lure other children into sexual victimization. Whether or not the boy realizes he is being used sexually or taken advantage of will sometimes depend on the expertise or subtlety of the seducer and the level of maturation, sophistication, and knowledge of the victim. Often this victim will experience confusion in regard to an awareness of what is happening and how to handle the situation.

Entrapment

The offender may take advantage of or even lure the victim into a compromising situation and then extort sex through blackmail. For example, having allowed or even encouraged the boy to engage in some type of forbidden behavior, such as smoking "pot" or looking at some pornography, he now approaches the boy sexually, knowing the boy will neither refuse nor tell, lest his own misbehavior be discovered by the police or his parents.

These are all variations on the techniques of persuasion, and in any given case a number of such strategies may be employed. When this is the form the victimization takes, there may be a resulting feeling of compliance, cooperation, or even collaboration on the part of the victim that makes it difficult for him not to feel partly responsible for what has transpired. Because of the *way* the boy was victimized he may not have experienced it as a transgression or even regard himself as a victim.

> *My first real sexual experience happened when I was 12 years old. This [25-year old] guy gave me a blow job and I remember it felt really good. Looking back, that good sexual feeling contributed to my thinking that I was doing this **with** him instead of his doing this to me. I remember being afraid "we" would get caught. At the time I didn't see myself as a victim because I had enjoyed the sex act. I thought of it as something we had done together—not something he had done to me. Years later I was troubled by the fact that I had enjoyed the sex, that I had had an orgasm. I was having sexual problems with my girlfriend at the time and I used to worry that maybe I was gay and just hadn't come to terms with it.*

One of the critical recovery tasks then may be helping him differentiate cooperation from consent and separating acceptance from approval.

> *What this guy would do is give me a list of different sexual acts and tell me to select among them and choose one. I felt I had to make a choice. I would pick the least offensive behavior to survive but I still felt responsible since I was the one to make the decision.*

Coercion Techniques

Coercion techniques involve compelling the victim to submit to and/or perform some undesired sexual act under the implied or expressed threat of personal harm or under conditions that preclude resistance.

28

Incapacitation

The offender may render the victim helpless through chemical or physical means or access a victim already in a condition of diminished resistance or unconsciousness. For example, the offender may sexually fondle a victim who is asleep or may drug the victim or ply him with alcohol until the person is intoxicated or has passed out and then take advantage of him sexually.

Authority

The offender may use his position of authority over a subordinate to compel him to engage in sex. For example, a father may use his authority over his son both as an adult and as a parent to demand sex from a child who believes he cannot defy his father's orders. Or a parole officer may threaten to revoke a boy's parole unless he engages in sex with the officer.

Verbal Threat

The offender may verbally express some intention to harm, injure, or inflict some other adverse consequence on the victim himself or on someone else emotionally close to him in order to make the victim submit sexually. For example, an offender may threaten to harm a young boy's pet unless he complies with the sexual demands.

Intimidation

The offender may instill fear of resistance on the part of his victim by brandishing a weapon or calling attention to his formidable size or ominous reputation. For example, an offender may engage one or more cohorts to outnumber his victim, or he may make his victim submit by pointing a gun at him.

Physical Force

The offender may use his physical strength to overpower his victim and overcome his resistance. For example, an offender may physically attack his victim, subdue him, and sexually assault him. The actual extent of physical force used in the assault may range from minimal restraint to extreme brutality in such cases.

These are all various forms of coercion, any combination of which may occur in a particular case. When this is the strategy employed by the perpetrator, the victim may have more of a sense of being sexually abused or transgressed against. Feelings of fear, helplessness, and a sense of endangerment may have predominated in a psychological state of crisis during his victimization.

I was hitchhiking home from a high school dance. A guy offered me a ride. We weren't talking, just driving, when suddenly he grabbed my left hand and started pulling it toward his groin area. I tried to pull back, but he was strong and I couldn't do it. I just froze. I got really scared. He kept holding my hand between his legs and I could feel that he had an erection. Then he let my wrist go and began to grope me. I pushed his hand away and jumped out of the car. I got bruised from hitting the street, but I didn't break any bones or anything. What frightened me about this incident was that I felt my life was on the line. I thought that the guy was crazy, that there was definitely something wrong with him. He was a big guy and I felt helpless. I think I had a vision of me being kidnapped. I thought of him as a person who was going to do me in.

The victim who is coerced may feel more psychologically vanquished and devastated from the assault. Nevertheless, since males are expected to maintain control over their lives under all circumstances, the male victim of coerced sex might still fault himself for not successfully preventing the assault.

A woman isn't expected to be stronger than a male assailant, so it's no reflection on her if he overpowers her and she fails to resist the assault, but for a man it's different. It's a humiliation to get beaten and an even greater disgrace to be used sexually.

Chapter Four

The Relationship of the Offender to the Victim

Another aspect of the sexual victimization that needs to be explored is the nature of the relationship that existed between the offender and the victim prior to the sexual abuse. What role did the offender play in the victim's life?

The offender may have been a complete stranger and, therefore, exists in the victim's life only in the context of the offense. Little or nothing may be otherwise known about him. More often, however, the victim will have been acquainted with his victimizer in some fashion. The offender may be a casual acquaintance, a close friend or associate, a person who occupies a legitimate role in the victim's life (such as babysitter, teacher, clergyman, or employer), or a relative or family member. The clinician needs to explore with the victim how he felt about the perpetrator—not how he felt about what the perpetrator did sexually, but how the victim felt about him as a person. What did the offender mean to the victim prior to the sexual abuse? How did the victim feel toward him? Did he like this person? Was this someone whose company the victim enjoyed? How had he been treated by the offender? What did he mean to his perpetrator?

An offender, like any human being, possesses both positive and negative qualities, strengths and weaknesses. You will find that preoffense relationships between perpetrator and victim range from close emotional bonding with genuine and mutual affection to relationships characterized by hate, fear, and distrust. One of the ways this can be approached is by asking the victim, *"Suppose the relationship between you and [the offender] were exactly the same as it existed, except that he never sexually abused you at all. How would you feel about him then?"*

Essentially you are trying to ascertain how the victim regards the perpetrator as a person. Here you are helping the victim to separate the offender from the offense and to differentiate between what the offender meant to him and what the offense meant to him. It may help clarify what was more significant to the victim: the offender or the victimization. On the one hand, where there has been a close emotional bond with the perpetrator, the significance of the victimization may be minimized. As human beings we tend to excuse behaviors of persons we care about that we would not tolerate in those whom we don't like. On the other hand, where the sexual transgression itself predominates, the victim may experience a betrayal as more devastating if it is by a friend than if it is by someone who meant nothing to him. There may be different reactions to the victimization then, depending on the meaning of the offender to the victim.

In order for the victim to process this experience, his clinician must also be capable of separating the offender from the offense. Unfortunately, some human service providers have difficulty doing this. Since the offense is a despicable act, they regard its perpetrator as a despicable person. Recognizing the serious and harmful nature of sexual victimization, they attribute the perpetrator's offense to willful irresponsibility and malicious intent. Knowing no one would choose to be victimized, they may approach their client with the assumption that this victim does not like his victimizer and with the attitude that the victim *should* not like his abuser. This, in our view, is a serious error. It may inhibit the victim from revealing his actual feelings or he may feel the need to censor his disclosures. For example, we have a boy in grammar school who was molested by a male teacher to whom he was very attached. In listening to the boy talk positively about this man, his interviewer (who did not know the offender) nevertheless felt compelled to "correct" the boy's impression of his teacher by saying: *"This man was not your friend. Friends don't do the kinds of things he did to persons they really care about. He was just being friendly toward you in order to take advantage of you. Anything that he did that appeared nice was just a way to trick you. This was his way of making you feel obligated to him so he could take advantage of you sexually. He is not a nice man. He's done bad things."*

Where does this leave the child? It may leave him feeling *"this interviewer doesn't really understand, and I must protect my friend [by recanting]."* Or *"If this is what the interviewer thinks of my friend, then what does this interviewer think of me, since I did the same things?"* Or *"I have to agree with this interviewer and tell him what he wants to hear—he won't listen otherwise—so I'll say, 'Yes, I dislike this teacher. I went along with him because I was scared of him. I really hate him and I never want to see him again'."* And he doesn't want to see him because he feels guilty about betraying a friend and now doesn't want to face him or fears this teacher will be angry at him, blame him, and not like him anymore. Or *"this interviewer must be right, so this means I am really stupid to be so easily fooled by someone I knew and trusted."*

By **reacting** rather than **responding,** the human service provider may preclude the victim's processing the experience. A more helpful response might be, *"Although I don't actually know this teacher, it seems like he did a lot of nice things for you. He paid attention to you. He helped you with your homework. He took you to some nice places like the movies and the zoo. He bought you some nice presents. He made you feel welcome at his home and let you use his swimming pool or play video games on his television set. You know, I can understand how you might like this teacher very much. I can understand your wanting to go over to his home as often as possible. It seems like he did a lot of nice things for you."* And if it seems important at this time to focus on the offense behavior, you could go on to say, *"But you know something? Your friend is not in trouble for all the good things he did. He's in trouble because he did some things that are against the law. He did some things with you that grown-ups are not allowed to do with children—that's why he's in trouble. Sometimes good people do wrong things. Anybody can make a mistake—even teachers."*

Approaching the matter in this fashion gives the victim an opportunity to examine how he does feel about his perpetrator. It permits the victim to acknowledge any positive feelings he may have for the perpetrator that he may be hesitant to express otherwise, believing that such feelings would be improper or might be misunderstood.

If the offender was a stranger, then of course there was no preexisting emotional relationship and the perpetrator, as a person, may remain an enigma in the psychological experience of the victim. The reaction to the offender, then, may reflect the victim's understanding of and reaction to the offense. How he feels about being victimized will often characterize how he feels about his victimizer. This would also tend to be the case where the preexisting relationship was very casual or neutral.

If the preexisting relationship was negative, the victimization may be experienced as further reason to dislike the perpetrator and as confirming the perpetrator's worthlessness. If, however, the preexisting relationship was a positive one, coming to terms with the abuse may be more difficult. Some victims will deny or minimize the significance of the victimization or accept it as the price they must pay to maintain the relationship. For others it will diminish the value of the relationship or lead them to become more ambivalent in their feelings toward the offender. For some it may irrevocably damage or end the emotional attachment or reverse it from a positive one into a negative one.

Although these are common directional trends, in actuality the victim may fluctuate between them, feeling one way at one point and differently at another time. Similarly, the course of the preexisting relationship also may have taken different turns. It would be helpful in examining the meaning of the preexisting relationship to ask the victim, *"Did it ever change in any important way on the part of either person at any time?"* If so, *"When did it change?" "How did it change?" "Why did it change?" "Did it change before the sexual victimization?" "Did it change during the sexual victimization? "Did it change after the sexual victimization in any way?"* If so, *"In what way did it change?"*

It is important that the clinician proceed in a neutral and dispassionate fashion with the focus on eliciting the victim's thoughts, feelings, and reactions to the experience. After you have explored how the victim regarded his perpetrator and how he regarded what actually transpired sexually between them you are ready to explore the next aspect of processing the victimization: how the victim experienced the sexual activity that occurred.

Chapter Five

The Nature of the Sexual Activity

One of the major aspects of sexual abuse is the actual sexual behavior that occurred during the victimization. We need to examine what took place and what responses occurred on the part of the victim. Generally speaking, at least in the initial phases, it is the perpetrator who is directing what occurs sexually. The sexual activity is not unfamiliar to him, and he has an awareness of its destination. He is sexually experienced, whereas this may not be true for the victim. It may be the victim's introduction to sex, and he may not have had any conventional, consenting, age-appropriate prior sexual experiences. He then lacks a base for comparison and a framework by which to process or evaluate what is occurring. The task here is to help the victim explore what he experienced sexually. What has he discovered about the nature of his sexuality and how does he understand what has transpired?

In addressing sexual assault where the victim and perpetrator are both males, the task for the clinician is to be able to recognize and validate the victim's fear, anger, and concern in this regard without endorsing or reinforcing homophobic attitudes on his or society's part. One way of doing this is to reinterpret the meaning of the experience in regard to the dynamics of aggression rather than of sexuality, clarifying the issues of coercion or compliance versus consent. However, when the key concern of the client is that the victimization was in a same-sex context and what is particularly disturbing for him is that the sexual activity involved another male, then a number of issues in regard to sexuality will need to be addressed. The basic question such clients have is, *"What does this mean about my sexuality?"* with underlying concerns such as, *"Am I gay?"* or *"Will I now become homosexual?"*

> *It was like if you had sex with someone that has venereal disease and you are afraid you are going to get that disease. If you have sex with someone who is homosexual, even though you didn't want the sex, you are afraid that you are going to catch it. I was afraid that it was going to spring up somewhere down the line. I was gang-raped when I was fourteen. Throughout the assault these guys kept saying that I liked it and that I really wanted it. I think that was the worst thing about it for me because it made me doubt myself. I knew that I didn't want them to do it, but I thought maybe I did something to make them think I did.*

Such concerns often seem to be raised by the nature of the male victim's sexual responses and reactions during the sexual victimization. A 28-year old male victim reflects on his molestation as a young adolescent:

> *I remember feeling guilty about getting an erection and later I saw that as evidence that maybe I must have really wanted him to do it. I also thought that this gave him the message that*

*I wanted it. I felt like it encouraged him: by getting an erection
I showed that I was interested.*

For such clients it can be helpful to identify a number of
interpretations that can be attached to such experiences, thus
allowing them to arrive at a fuller and more accurate understanding of the event.

Involuntary Erection

The male victim's sexual worries may derive in part from his
fear that experiencing an erection and ejaculation during his
victimization indicates unrealized desire for such activity on
his part. The fact is that males experience erections under
a number of circumstances besides sexual arousal. For example, a male may awake from sleep with an erection even
though he was not experiencing an erotic dream. Males can
get erections when they are sexually aroused, but they can
also get erections when they are not sexually stimulated—
most males can recall experiencing an erection, realizing they
were not feeling sexually aroused at the time, and wondering
to themselves, *"Why am I getting hard?"* It appears to be
a physiological experience unaccompanied by any sexually
arousing mental state.

Erections can accompany such mood states as boredom,
fatigue, anger, depression, and anxiety. Sometimes a victim
is confused about experiencing an erection in the context of
stress associated with his being victimized, believing that a
male cannot "get it up" if he is feeling scared or anxious. This
is a curious notion since most men can recall a situation in
which their erection would not diminish, even though they
were stressed—for example, having a "hard-on" in class and
then being asked to stand up and answer a question.

In the context of the sexual abuse, then, the client may experience a spontaneous erection or one in response to direct physical stimulation. Whatever the situation, sexual *arousal* and sexual *desire* are separate issues—a person may not *desire* a sexual experience even though he may be *aroused* by it.

Ejaculation and Orgasm

Ejaculation, too, is a physiological response. Since ejaculation is frequently accompanied by orgasm the two experiences are often blurred in the individual's mind, but they are not identical even though both are commonly referred to by the same slang term, "coming off." *Ejaculation* refers to the sudden physiological discharge of seminal fluid from the penis, and *orgasm* refers to an intense emotional rush of erotic excitement and pleasure. Either may occur involuntarily as a result of genital manipulation and stimulation. Ejaculation and orgasm may occur within the context of erotic passion and desire, but they also can occur where passion and desire are nonexistent.

It is characteristic of many sex offenders to attempt to *elicit* a sexual response from their victims by performing masturbation, fellatio, or the like on them. This serves a number of purposes in the psychology of the offender. He may see this as confirmation of his **power** and **control:** *"I am in more control of this guy's sexual responses than he is himself."* He may believe that this indicates sexual enjoyment on the part of the victim: *"You know you like it; you're getting 'hot'."* This may lead the offender to think that the victim will be less likely to view the experience as an unwanted assault, less likely to disclose it to others, and perhaps more receptive to a continuing sexual involvement. If the victim does report the assault to the authorities, the offender may think that the sexual response will make the victim less credible in their eyes.

The victim himself may not know what to make of his experiencing an erection, ejaculation, and/or orgasm in response to the sexual victimization. He needs to differentiate sexual **activity** from sexual **object** or sexual **desire**. What he may find out during the sexual victimization is that he, like most persons, finds manual or oral sex stimulating. He discovers this in a context where another male is the source of such stimulation—this does not necessarily mean that he finds *males* sexually appealing. It may only mean he finds oral sex, for example, to be pleasurable. It is the **activity** (getting sucked), not the **object** (the person sucking him), to which he responds sexually. It does not necessarily follow that because he **can** be aroused in this fashion, he **chooses** to be sexually active in this way. In fact, as one of our clients once stated: *"I resented the fact that he could do this to me, that he could get me 'off'."*

Masturbation Fantasy

Another concern the clinician should anticipate is that the victim may find his subsequent masturbatory fantasies focused on the coerced sexual activity, or that the victimization incident may intrude into his consenting sexual activity.

> *I would be in the middle of a fantasy or something, and all of a sudden this guy [the perpetrator] would flash across my mind, and I'd think: "Oh, my God!" It was oral sex with him doing me, and I would think: "Oh, I want to get out of this thought. I don't like this idea." If I was in the middle of masturbation, Bam! That was it. I'd lose my concentration. I'd worry about*

it, kind of like "Wow! What does this mean?" Most guys don't have this thought.

He may fear that the nature of his sexuality has been altered by the victimization. The clinician can point out that this may actually reflect an effort at mastery of the traumatic event on the part of the client rather than an alteration in his sexual orientation. When he was being sexually victimized, someone else was in control of him sexually. During masturbation he is literally in control of himself sexually, and this may be a way in which he attempts to reclaim mastery over his own sexuality. Likewise, his participation in consensual sex reflects his choice and decision.

However, since both activities are sexual ones, it is not unusual or surprising that this might trigger flashbacks in his mind to previous unsettling sexual events. The fantasy thoughts are prompted by fear more than desire, by anxiety more than pleasure. Although this may indicate that the person is still recovering from the experience of sexual victimization—that there is still some unfinished business in this regard—these are normal reactions to an unusual experience. It does not necessarily mean that his sexuality has been put in jeopardy.

The purpose of processing these sexual details of the victimization is to help the client understand that reactions commonly experienced in this context may be the result of dynamics other than unrecognized or latent homosexual desires. However, you should not, through overreassurance, convey to the client an emphatic denial that he is homosexual because he in fact may be—*not* because his sexual victimization altered his orientation, but because in the context of being sexually victimized he *discovered* his homosexuality. By strongly communicating that there is some other explanation for his responses—any explanation other than that he is gay—you are implicitly condemning his actual sexual nature. Here you need to be clear that it is not the *sexuality* but the *lack of consent* that is objectionable in regard to sexual abuse. However, discovering one is gay in a homophobic society is often traumatic in itself, and the clinician needs to consider beforehand how he can be of help should this discovery emerge in the context of addressing sexual abuse. If the clinician is unknowledgeable or inexperienced in counseling gay clients, he should refer his client to other resources for this issue.

Chapter Six

The Frequency of the Sexual Victimization

Another feature of the victimization to be explored is the *frequency* of contact. Was this a single event or were there repeated contacts over time? If so, how often and over what period of time? Have there been multiple episodes of sexual victimization at various points throughout the individual's life? If so, were these simultaneous, sequential, or both?

If the victim's assault was a single episode, he may be more able to discount it and distance himself from it as an unfortunate, external, life event. (However one must not assume, simply because it happened once, that the victim *should* discount it.) Whereas if he has been victimized a number of times, he may experience this as some reflection on himself, asking: *"Why does this keep happening to me? What am I doing wrong?"*

Younger or sexually naive males might express some concerns about their masculinity—understanding that guys are attracted to girls, *"Did this guy [the perpetrator] think that I was a girl? Do I look like a girl or act like one?"* It may be helpful in such cases to explain that although most men are attracted to females and females their own age, some are not. Some men are attracted to children, and some of them specifically to boys. Although we see such persons as grown-ups, sometimes in some ways they still feel like children themselves. *"This guy picked you not because he thought you looked like a girl, but because you look like and act just like what you in fact are, a real boy. Maybe you are the kind of boy he himself would like to have been when he was your age, or you are the kind of boy he would like to have had as a friend—but it is because you are a boy that he picked you."*

The concern with older or less naïve victims might be their appearance or gender identity: *"Why do guys keep coming on to me sexually? Do I look gay? Do they recognize something about me that I don't recognize in myself?"* Many people in fact fail to distinguish between **homosexuality** (sexual attraction to age mates of the same sex) and **pedophilia** (sexual attraction to children) and subscribe to the mistaken belief that male homosexuals will molest young boys. The male victim, realizing that his perpetrator is also a male, may mistakenly conclude that the offender is gay. It may be helpful for the clinician to explain that most people are sexually drawn to partners of the same age, but some persons have cross-generational sexual attractions, that is, they are sexually attracted to children in addition to, or instead of, persons their own age. In fact, homosexual males pose no more risk of sexual abuse to underage boys than heterosexual males pose to underage girls. Persons who do pose such a risk are properly known as **pedophiles.** When explaining to a young victim why some men try to take advantage of him you might say, *"The reason you are approached has more to do with your age than your sex."*

It should be noted here that since the underage male victim often mistakenly assumes his perpetrator is gay, he may subsequently misdirect his resulting fear and anger toward homosexuals, and the resulting homophobia may be symptomatic of having been sexually abused. But in a homophobic society this frequently gets masked and may be overlooked as an indicator that this male could have been a victim of same-sex assault.

When repetitive sexual contact has been occurring continuously for some time, the victim will have had to psychologically accommodate this fact and may not be clear as to how this has affected his sexual development. Examples of resulting altered sexual activity might be the following:

- He may take to initiating sexual contact with others as an attempt to reclaim control in sexual encounters.
- He may "cruise" other males sexually or prostitute himself as a way of asserting that he will determine when, under what conditions, and with whom he will have sex.
- He may be driven to compulsive and indiscriminate heterosexual pursuits and conquests as an attempt to reestablish his heterosexuality.
- He may put a premium on sexuality for self-worth or use sex as leverage in his relationships to get what he wants.
- He may move from victim to victimizer, modeling what he has experienced.
- He may view it as a means of leveling *("I'm not the only*

one in this family who's going to be 'damaged goods'"), or as a means of reassurance (*"If my victim isn't being harmed by this, then I haven't been either."*).

Such offenses may constitute a post-traumatic stress reaction; it is not uncommon for the victim to replay the abuse scenario with himself now in control and the sexual experience not being unwanted but enjoyed.

In helping the victim to process the experience of being sexually abused, the clinician would want to inquire *"When did this begin in your life? How long did it go on? Tell me about the first time (or the first time you remember). Tell me about the next time. Tell me about any time that what occurred changed or was different. Tell me about the last time."* Where it was an ongoing involvement ask, *"Did it change in any way over time on [the perpetrator's] part and/or on your part?"*

Another dimension to the frequency of the sexual victimization is the **emotional intensity** that accompanied it. How erotically excited would the offender become during the sexual acts? Did the involvement have the intense quality of an obsession or compulsion? Was this experienced by the victim as very driven behavior on the part of the perpetrator? Did this cause concern for the victim in any way? What was the victim's emotional frame of mind during the sexual activity: fear, confusion, anger, excitement, love, etc.?

To what extent was the intensity of the sexual involvement reciprocal or unbalanced and what implications did this have for the victim? Was there an imbalance and, if so, in what regard: *"Did you feel he liked you more than you liked him [or vice-versa]?"* Was either person becoming jealous or possessive of the other? Was the offender falling in love with the victim? Was the victim falling in love with the offender? Or was the emotional connection a more neutral one with the primary focus on the sex itself? Or was it more a contest of wills, a power struggle around issues of domination and control? Again, did any of this change over time? You need then to examine how this came to an end (if it is not continuing at the present time). Who stopped it? Why did it stop (as you best understand or surmise the reason)? Did the victim want it to end? Did it end the way he wanted it to?

A sense of powerlessness or vulnerability may be reinforced in the victim when victimization continues over time. The ultimate response may be a sense of resignation. Alternatively the victim may have collaborated with the offender in sharing this forbidden activity, or he may have become resentful and increasingly rebellious. Such reactions may be manifested in the involvement with the perpetrator and/or they may be reflected in other aspects of the victim's sexual life adjustment as noted above.

Where the victimization did continue over time, what permitted it to continue? Either the victim, fearing unwanted repercussions, chose not to tell anyone, or revelation on his part did not result in effective intervention. This brings us to the issues of secrecy and disclosure.

Chapter Seven

Secrecy, Disclosure, or Discovery

Finally we come to the issue of secrecy, disclosure, or discovery in regard to the sexual victimization. In exploring this issue the clinician will want to ascertain how the victimization came to light. Was it *accidentally discovered* or was it *intentionally disclosed* by the victim? In the former situation you may encounter more denial on the part of the victim and more resistance to discussing the event. He may feel further victimized in that something he did not choose to disclose has been discovered about him and he may be an involuntary client. As previously noted, there are many reasons that would inhibit a male from reporting his victimization:

- He may not consider himself a victim.
- He may be enjoying the sexual experience.
- He may value the benefits associated with his victimization, such as money or drugs.
- He may care about his perpetrator and feel the need to protect him.

- He may feel embarrassed, guilty, or worried about what others will think or say.
- He may fear retaliation from the perpetrator or punishment from others.
- He may be concerned that no one will believe him. Etc.

How you respond to this client depends on what you understand to be his reasons for not telling. Perhaps one way to begin is to think of the client as a customer and ask, *"How may I help you?"* The starting place may be how he feels about this personal matter being discovered and the expectation that he will now discuss it.

If this is the first time the victim has intentionally disclosed this event to anyone, you need to clarify **why** he is telling about this now. What does he expect will result? If this is a past event in his life, why did he keep it secret and what has made him decide to reveal this now? Generally speaking, in the case of voluntary disclosure the client will be more forthcoming with information regarding the abuse, although he may censor some aspects until he feels safe in the counseling relationship.

Anticipatory guidance is one of the techniques we have found useful in working with victims who deny and as a means to communicate to the client that we do understand what he is going through and have his best interests at heart. By using this technique along with analogies and a light touch of humor we can convey to the client that we are allies in this process. In this technique, the clinician describes for the client what the client may already have experienced, as well as what he may come to experience in the future in regard to his sexual victimization. For example, an involuntary client may say that he doesn't want to talk about his victimization. Our response might be the following script:

That's okay. A lot of guys I have worked with have felt the same way—they didn't want to talk about it. They just wanted to forget it. I can understand that. You don't have to talk to me about it, but I would like to share some things with you about what I've learned from having worked with a good number of boys [or men] your age who were taken advantage of sexually. I'll do all the talking. What I would like you to do is to listen. If at any point you want to ask a question or make a comment, feel free to.

*One of the things I've learned is that the offender often makes a serious effort to sexually arouse the boy he is taking advantage of. He may attempt to do this by fondling the boy, or masturbating him, or performing oral sex on him. And usually he succeeds. I don't know if this is what your offender tried with you, but if so, that's not at all unusual. The boy gets an erection and that can be confusing to him. It's confusing because we are led to believe that if guys are under stress or uncomfortable, they will have a difficult time "getting it up." Now I don't know why we tend to believe this, because if we think about it most of us can remember the embarrassing experience of getting an erection in class—and sometimes we don't even know why we're getting a "hard on" because we're not, at the time, necessarily feeling "horny" or having any sexual thoughts. But we're getting an erection anyway, and the next thing we know the teacher is calling on us to stand up in class and answer a question, or come up to the front of the class and do a problem on the blackboard. And as embarrassing or uncomfortable as that can be, the erection won't go away—in fact sometimes it gets harder! So I don't know where we get the notion that stress will prevent an erection, but guys often think that it will and then become confused when the offender succeeds in eliciting an erection on their part. You know, actually it would be more unusual if the victim **didn't** get an erection since this is usually an involuntary and automatic response to physical stimulation.*

Not only does the offender usually elicit an erection from his victim, but he also succeeds in getting the guy "off" as well. He gets the guy to "come." Now we use the slang term "to come off" to mean a couple of things. Sometimes we use the term to mean ejaculation, which is shooting sperm and seminal fluid. And sometimes we use the term to mean orgasm, which is an emotional rush of pleasure or sexual climax that often accompanies ejaculation but not always. Sometimes guys ejaculate without having an orgasm. For example, usually guys can tell you of consenting sexual experiences they have had where, even though they wanted sex and could perform and they ejaculated, it wasn't very satisfying. It wasn't so hot. It wasn't good sex. In other words, they did not experience a very strong orgasm. Sometimes that's how it is for the guy being sexually victimized—he gets an erection, he "comes off," but it isn't highly pleasurable. He's uncomfortable with what's happening, and it's not an enjoyable experience for him sexually.

But for others guys the experience may be different. They do have an intense orgasm and then may be confused as to why something they really didn't want was so pleasurable. Well, sometimes the response is a result of the sexual skill and technique of the offender. He may be very expert in such activities—he gives good "head" for example. What may be unsettling for the boy, however, is the fact that the sex was so exciting or pleasurable; he may feel guilty about this or worry about what this may mean about his own sexuality.

*Well, first we need to understand that to be victimized **doesn't** mean the sexual experience had to be unpleasant. For example, drugs might produce a pleasant effect for the person who is abusing them. And, too, there is the matter of free choice—there are such things as "unwanted pleasures." I remember one guy saying to me that he resented the fact the offender could "get him off." In other words, even when the boy finds the sexual experience pleasurable, this is still victimization. The offender is subjecting the victim to an experience the victim either would not voluntarily choose to have with this person or, because the victim is underage, cannot give informed consent to.*

Oftentimes a boy who is disturbed to find that the victimization has been sexually pleasurable may worry whether this might mean he is gay or will become homosexual. Well, I don't know if you are gay or not—and if that is a concern we can explore it—but if you are asking, will this experience **make** you gay, the answer is "No." If experiences alone determined our sexually, we'd all be in love with our hands! In other words, most boys masturbate and find this to be pleasurable, but they don't worry about falling in love with their hands or that this will prevent them from developing other sexual interests.

When guys worry that their victimization experience will affect their sexual orientation, they usually are confusing the sexual activity with its source. What I mean is that they are discovering that what the offender **did,** the sexual **act** (let's say, oral sex) was pleasurable. They discover this in the context of another guy performing oral sex on them. This doesn't necessarily mean that they find other males sexually desirable. It's the **act** that "turns them on," not the **person.**

Sometimes guys have doubts about the nature of their sexuality because they find when they do masturbate they have disturbing thoughts or fantasies about the victimization experience. Again, this is not an unusual experience. The thoughts and fantasies constitute **memories**—they don't necessarily reflect unacknowledged desires or wishes. When someone is victimizing you they are in control of your sexuality. When you masturbate yourself you are in control of your own sexuality, but the activity may correspond to what the offender did (that is, he masturbated you), so the memory of the event returns or you flash back to it. This is serving the purpose of reclaiming sexual control in regard to the event. Most likely this will subside with time and later be replaced with other, more comfortable, memories.

Now we learn from our experiences, and one of the things sexual victimization can teach us is there are guys in this world who would like to perform sexual acts on boys or other males. So if you want some quick and easy sex—like getting a "blow job"—it's easy to find. No commitment, no relationship, just impersonal sexual release—quick, easy, inexpensive gratification. Not only that *but maybe some other "perks" as well, such as money or drugs in exchange for letting the guy service you. In other words, sometimes guys who have been sexually victimized find later they may be going out "looking for it" but then wonder if they're "cruising" because they've "turned gay." The returning for further sexual contact or seeking out similar sexual encounters usually serves a number of purposes that we can examine if this is of interest to you. But in general we find it is another way of reclaiming sexual control over one's life: "I'll now decide when and where and with whom this will happen. I can use someone sexually like I was used."*

Most often, in our experience, we find that the client will make intermittent responses throughout this narration. However, even if clients do not say very much about their own victimization, we usually note that their body language seems to register some relief: they seem less tense, make more eye contact, even smile at times, and breathe more comfortably. Knowledge is power, and the more they understand the more empowered they feel to deal with what happened.

In helping the male victim cognitively reframe his sexual experience, however, it is very important *not* to give the message: *"Don't worry. None of this means you are gay. There is some alternative explanation for what you experienced—you don't have to worry about **that** terrible thing."* For this would imply that being gay is not acceptable and would reinforce all the homophobic messages delivered by our society. First, being overly reassuring often has a paradoxical effect on the client, but even more important, what if the client *is* gay—not because the assault **made** him gay but because he discovered his homosexuality in the context of being victimized? If that is the case, then you have to explore what being gay means to him. What are his attitudes and values in this regard; where did he acquire these? What are his realistic options? Is he going to pursue his inclinations or not? Does he want to live a celibate or chaste (nonsexual) life and, if so, is that possible? Is he considering suicide? Can he differentiate between sexuality and character (see above, page 18). Guidelines for addressing this issue are beyond the scope of this text, but we raise this possibility here so that persons working with male victims can anticipate what might emerge in this context and make some thoughtful preparation and contingency plans for handling this discussion, should it arise.

Obviously the way you approach the sexual experiences will to some extent depend on the age and sexual development of the victim. When we are working with sexually mature and experienced males we choose to speak explicitly about sexual activities and experiences (as in the above example of **anticipatory guidance**). When we are working with preadolescent, sexually immature, or inexperienced males we often choose nonsexual examples or analogies to make our points. For example, with young children we find the analogy to tickling a useful one:

Have you ever had the experience of being tickled and not wanting it or liking it, but you still laughed? Sure. You see, just because you laughed didn't mean you wanted to be tickled or enjoyed being tickled, did it? Was there ever a time that you were tickled and you enjoyed it? Sure. And you giggled and laughed, didn't you, and had a good time? Would you laugh when another boy tickled you? Sure. Would you laugh when a girl tickled you? Sure. What was making you laugh? It was the tickling—not who was doing it. It was the tickling that felt good.

To get across the idea that something enjoyable might nevertheless not be good for you, we could use an analogy to food:

Candy tastes good, doesn't it? And yet it might not be good for you. It can cause cavities, or upset your tummy, or make you fat. So not everything that tastes good (or feels good) is always good for you to have (or to do).

Values clarification in regard to sexual victimization is often necessary: What was wrong about this event was not that it was **sexual** activity between two males; it was the **exploitation** that was wrong. The taking advantage of someone else is what made it an offense. With young victims the message they usually hear is that "**sex is bad**" or "**sex is wrong.**" In addressing this we might say:

*If someone steals some money from you, is it the money that's bad? No, it's the stealing that's wrong. So whether another person steals money from you, or friendship, or sex, it is the **stealing** that makes it bad.*

In a sex-negative society like ours, obviously the child will be getting many powerful messages that communicate that sex itself is bad. Just as in this homophobic society males will receive many powerful messages that sexual contact with other males is bad. Although we realize that expressing a different view may not, in itself, change the client's attitudes, we think it is important to speak out lest silence imply agreement on our part. In so doing we expose the client to the fact that there are other views on this matter. We hope that this will ultimately aid him in determining the truth of this matter for himself.

Chapter Eight

Conclusion

In dealing with the complex subject of human sexual behavior, it is important to separate out such issues as whether the sexual behavior is *morally* right or wrong, *legally* allowed or prohibited, *psychologically* harmless or harmful, *physically* safe or dangerous, and *sexually* pleasurable or not pleasurable. Although separate, these issues may overlap in some instances. As clinicians we tend to address primarily psychological issues, but in working with a victim of sexual abuse we may find that we are required to address the abuse from other perspectives as well. It is helpful to point out when the client is raising an issue that is different from a clinical one: *"What you are asking is a medical question"*; or, *"What you are expressing is a religious belief"*; or, *"What you are raising is a legal issue"*; etc.

Insofar as the issue departs from scientific knowledge and empirical study, you are entering—as we have in this text—the realm of attitudes and views, a realm in which there are as yet no definitive answers and where opinion (one hopes informed) predominates.

Recovery

The goal of clinical intervention in the case of male sexual victimization is to help the client achieve a sense of mastery over the troubling event: to arrive at a place where he neither denies the abuse nor is mentally preoccupied with it, where memories of the trauma are no longer intolerable, and where the disruptive impact of the event and its upsetting intrusion into the psychological functioning of the client have diminished. This is achieved through clinical interventions that help the client process and clarify the experience; validate his responses, reactions, and concerns; and provide information, values clarification, and alternative means of resolution.

Now in my life when, for some reason, I think about this—about what happened—it is really something gone by. The distress and upset have gone away. On my right thigh I have a scar. When I was ten years old I cut myself there by accident with a jackknife. The scar is there and when I notice it I remember the injury, but the wound healed a long time ago—there is no pain now. That's how I feel about having been sexually abused. It's not something I'll forget, but it doesn't bother me anymore.

Adult Male Sexual Victimization Questionnaire

Sexual Victimization Questionnaire

We are interested in learning more about the kinds of sexual abuse, trauma, or victimization males experience in their lives. This is a very sensitive issue and, therefore, not a great deal is known about it. We would like to ask you to help by filling out this questionnaire. Many of the questions are very personal, but it is important to be as truthful as you can in order for us to be able to be of help.

Instructions

There are a number of ways in which a male can be sexually victimized:

1. **Witness:** *He may witness disturbing sexual activity on the part of another person.* For example, seeing an older person expose himself/herself and masturbate in front of him; witnessing his

father engage in incest with his sister; watching his mother engage in sexual activity with a number of men; or seeing someone get raped.

2. **Advances:** *He may have someone make unwanted sexual advances toward him which—although he is able to resist or escape—he finds frightening, disturbing, or upsetting.* For example, someone offers him a ride when he is hitchhiking and puts his hand on his leg or touches his genitals; an older person sexually propositions him; or in jail someone offers him protection in exchange for sex. Whatever the situation, it was one in which either the victim was able to get away or the offender finally took "no" for an answer.

3. **Pressure:** *He may be pressured or manipulated into engaging in unwanted sexual activity.* For example, through tricks, bribes, blackmail, or by making him feel obligated the offender takes sexual advantage of him; or he may be pressured into sexual activity as part of an initiation to join a club or gang or to become a member of a group.

4. **Force:** *He may be forced to submit to unwanted sexual activity.* For example, the offender gets sexual access to him by drugging him or getting him drunk, threatening him with injury, intimidating him with a weapon, or physically overpowering and attacking him.

5. **Other Trauma:** In addition, there are other, less direct ways in which a male may be sexually victimized or traumatized. For example, he may be humiliated or ridiculed in some sexual fashion (for example, a father might punish his son by making him wear girls' clothes); or he may be punished or maltreated for normal sexual behavior (for example, he may be beaten by his parents for masturbating).

We would like you to think back about your own life to see if any such things may have happened to you at any time. If something like this did, determine which category of experience (*witness, advances, pressure, force, other*) best describes what happened in order to determine where to list it. Often a person may experience more than one type of sexual victimization, so it will be important that you answer the questions for each and every section that applies to you.

Part A: WITNESS

1. Did you ever witness any sexual activity on the part of another person which troubled, upset, distressed, or disturbed you?

   ☐ YES   ☐ NO   ☐ DON'T KNOW

   [If your answer is NO or DON'T KNOW, skip to Part B.]

   a) What type of sexual activity did you witness? (Check all that apply.)

      ☐ *Indecent exposure:* someone sexually exposed himself/herself to you.

☐ *Masturbation:* someone masturbated himself/herself in your presence.

☐ *Heterosexual relations:* you witnessed male and female persons engaged in sexual activity together.

☐ *Homosexual relations:* you witnessed persons of the same sex engaged in sexual activity together.

☐ *Incest:* you witnessed family members (brother-sister, father-daughter, etc.) engaged in sexual relations with each other.

☐ *Sexual assault:* you heard or saw someone being raped or sexually assaulted.

☐ *Other* (Specify): _____

b) Describe the event(s) you witnessed. Whom did it involve and what did you observe? ____

_____

_____

_____

A-2

2. How old were you when this occurred? (If you don't know for sure, what would you guess your age to have been?) _____

3. How old was the other person(s)? (If you don't know for sure, what would you guess their age(s) to have been?) _____

4. What was the sex of the other person(s)?

   ☐ MALE   ☐ FEMALE   ☐ BOTH

5. What was the relationship of that person to you (for example, parent, relative, friend, acquaintance, babysitter, teacher, scout leader, neighbor, stranger, etc.)? _____

6. How many *different* times did something like this happen to you in your life? _____

7. Describe how you felt at the time this happened in regard to the following:

   a) Did you find this experience in any way *sexually pleasurable?*

      ☐ NO, not at all.
      ☐ YES, somewhat.
      ☐ YES, very much.
      ☐ Don't know.

b) Did you find this experience in any way *interesting*?

☐ NO, not at all.
☐ YES, somewhat.
☐ YES, very much.
☐ Don't know.

c) Did you find this experience in any way *exciting*?

☐ NO, not at all.
☐ YES, somewhat.
☐ YES, very much.
☐ Don't know.

d) Did you find this experience in any way *confusing*?

☐ NO, not at all.
☐ YES, somewhat.
☐ YES, very much.
☐ Don't know.

e) Did you find this experience in any way *frightening*?

☐ NO, not at all.
☐ YES, somewhat.
☐ YES, very much.
☐ Don't know.

f) Did you feel *depressed* about this happening?

☐ NO, not at all.
☐ YES, somewhat.
☐ YES, very much.
☐ Don't know.

g) Did you feel *upset* about this happening?

☐ NO, not at all.
☐ YES, somewhat.
☐ YES, very much.
☐ Don't know.

h) Did you feel *guilty* about this happening?

☐ NO, not at all.
☐ YES, somewhat.
☐ YES, very much.
☐ Don't know.

i) Did you feel this experience to be in any way *disgusting*?

☐ NO, not at all.
☐ YES, somewhat.
☐ YES, very much.
☐ Don't know.

j) Did you feel *angry* about this happening?

☐ NO, not at all.
☐ YES, somewhat.
☐ YES, very much.
☐ Don't know.

k) Did you feel *helpless*?

☐ NO, not at all.
☐ YES, somewhat.
☐ YES, very much.
☐ Don't know.

l) Were there any *other* feelings you had at the time in regard to this incident?
If so, what were they? _____

_____

_____

8. What was the most troubling part of this experience for you? _____

_____

_____

_____

9. Was there anything you liked or enjoyed about this experience at the time or anything you got out of it?

☐ YES   ☐ NO   ☐ DON'T KNOW

If *YES*, what was that? _____

_____

10. Did you tell anyone about this at the time?

☐ YES   ☐ NO

[If NO, skip to question 11.]

Please answer the following:

a) Whom did you tell? _____

b) What were your reasons for telling? That is, what did you want to happen or what did you expect this person to do? _____

_____

_____

_____

c) How did the person you told react? What did they do? _____

_____

_____

d) Was this person's response mostly:

☐ HELPFUL = made things better for the most part.

☐ HARMFUL = made things worse for the most part.

☐ INEFFECTUAL = neither made things better nor worse.

11. When this happened, did anyone find out about it in some way without your telling?

☐ YES   ☐ NO

[If NO, skip to question 12.]

a) Who found out? _____

b) How did they discover this? _____

_____

_____

c) What was their reaction? What did they do? _____

_____

_____

d) Was this person's response mostly:

☐ HELPFUL = made things better for the most part.

☐ HARMFUL = made things worse for the most part.

☐ INEFFECTUAL = neither made things better nor worse.

12. If *NO*, Why didn't you tell anyone at the time? _____

_____

_____

13. How serious or significant an event was this in regard to its effect on your life? How would you rate it on a scale from 1 (*unimportant*) to 10 (*extremely serious*)? _____

Part B: ADVANCES

1. Did anyone ever make unwanted sexual advances (verbal and/or physical) to you which you were able to decline or resist but which you found disturbing or troublesome?

    ☐ YES   ☐ NO   ☐ DON'T KNOW

    [If your answer is NO or DON'T KNOW, skip to Part C.]

2. What type of sexual advances did he/she make? (Check all that apply:)

    ☐ VERBAL = made suggestive remarks or "hit" on you, or propositioned you by offering something in exchange for sex.

    ☐ PHYSICAL = put his/her hands on an intimate part of your body (thighs, buttocks, genitals, etc.)

    Describe the circumstances and explain how this happened (that is, what the offender said or did, what he/she wanted, and what you said or did). _____

    _____

    _____

3. How old were you the first time something like this happened to you? (If you don't know for

sure, what would you guess your age to have been?) _____

4. How old was the other person(s)? (If you don't know for sure, what would you guess his/her age to have been?) _____

5. What was the sex of the other person(s)?

    ☐ MALE   ☐ FEMALE   ☐ BOTH

6. What was the relationship of that person to you (for example, parent, relative, friend, acquaintance, babysitter, teacher, scout leader, neighbor, stranger, etc.)? _____

7. How many *different* times did something like this happen to you in your life? _____

8. Was this experience disturbing or troublesome to you in any way?

    ☐ YES   ☐ NO

    If *YES*, explain: _____

    _____

    _____

    _____

9. Describe how you felt at the time this happened in regard to the following:

a) Did you find this experience in any way *sexually pleasurable*?

   ☐ NO, not at all.
   ☐ YES, somewhat.
   ☐ YES, very much.
   ☐ Don't know.

b) Did you find this experience in any way *interesting*?

   ☐ NO, not at all.
   ☐ YES, somewhat.
   ☐ YES, very much.
   ☐ Don't know.

c) Did you find this experience in any way *exciting*?

   ☐ NO, not at all.
   ☐ YES, somewhat.
   ☐ YES, very much.
   ☐ Don't know.

d) Did you find this experience in any way *confusing*?

   ☐ NO, not at all.
   ☐ YES, somewhat.

☐ YES, very much.
☐ Don't know.

e) Did you find his experience in any way *frightening*?

☐ NO, not at all.
☐ YES, somewhat.
☐ YES, very much.
☐ Don't know.

f) Did you feel *depressed* about this happening?

☐ NO, not at all.
☐ YES, somewhat.
☐ YES, very much.
☐ Don't know.

g) Did you feel *upset* about this happening?

☐ NO, not at all.
☐ YES, somewhat.
☐ YES, very much.
☐ Don't know.

h) Did you feel *guilty* about this happening?

☐ NO, not at all.
☐ YES, somewhat.
☐ YES, very much.
☐ Don't know.

i) Did you feel this experience to be in any way *disgusting*?

☐ NO, not at all.
☐ YES, somewhat.
☐ YES, very much.
☐ Don't know.

j) Did you feel *angry* about this happening?

☐ NO, not at all.
☐ YES, somewhat.
☐ YES, very much.
☐ Don't know.

k) Did you feel *helpless*?

☐ NO, not at all.
☐ YES, somewhat.
☐ YES, very much.
☐ Don't know.

1) Were there any *other* feelings you had at the time in regard to this incident? If so, what were they? _____

_____

_____

_____

10. What was the most troubling part of this experience for you? _____

_____

_____

_____

11. Was there anything you liked or enjoyed about this experience at the time or anything you got out of it?

☐ YES   ☐ NO   ☐ DON'T KNOW

If *YES*, what was that? _____

_____

_____

A-9

12. Did you tell anybody about this at the time?

☐ YES   ☐ NO

[If NO, skip to question 13.]

Please answer the following:

a) Whom did you tell? _____

b) What were your reasons for telling? That is, what did you want to happen or what did you expect this person to do? _____

_____

_____

c) How did the person you told react? What did they do? _____

_____

_____

d) Was this person's response mostly:

☐ HELPFUL = made things better for the most part.

☐ HARMFUL = made things worse for the most part.

☐ INEFFECTUAL = neither made things better nor worse.

13. When this happened, did anyone find out about it in some way without your telling?

☐ YES   ☐ NO

[If NO, skip to question 14.]

a) Who found out? _____

b) How did they discover this? _____

_____

_____

_____

c) What was their reaction? What did they do? _____

_____

_____

d) Was this person's response mostly:

☐ HELPFUL = made things better for the most part.

☐ HARMFUL = made things worse for the most part.

☐ INEFFECTUAL = neither made things better nor worse.

14. If *NO*, why didn't you tell anyone at the time? _____

_____

_____

Part C: PRESSURE

1. Were you ever pressured or manipulated into unwanted sexual activity in some fashion?

   ☐ YES   ☐ NO   ☐ DON'T KNOW

   [If your answer is NO or DON'T KNOW, skip to Part D.]

2. What means or strategies did the offender use to get you to participate? (Check all that apply.)

   ☐ DECEPTION = he/she tricked you into the sexual activity in some way.

   ☐ ENTICEMENT = he/she lured, bribed, or rewarded you in some fashion.

   ☐ ENTRAPMENT = he/she made you feel obligated or indebted to him/her in some way.

   ☐ EXTORTION = he/she blackmailed you or threatened to reveal some personally embarrassing or forbidden behavior on your part.

3. How did the offender get you to cooperate? Explain how this happened (how he/she manipulated, seduced, or pressured you into the sexual activity). _____

   _____

   _____

   _____

4. How old were you the first time something like this happened to you? (If you don't know for sure, what would you guess your age to have been?) _____

5. How old was the other person(s)? (If you don't know for sure, what would you guess his/her age to have been? _____

6. What was the sex of the other person(s)?

   ☐ MALE ☐ FEMALE ☐ BOTH

7. What was the relationship of that person to you (for example, parent, relative, friend, acquaintance, babysitter, teacher, scout leader, neighbor, stranger, etc.)? _____

_____

8. How long did this person's sexual involvement with you last? Over what period of time (days, weeks, months, years) did this sexual activity continue with him/her? _____

_____

9. How many times would you guess this person had sex with you in all? _____

10. Was this experience disturbing or troublesome to you in any way?

   ☐ YES ☐ NO

If *YES*, explain: _____

_____

_____

11. What type of sexual acts did the **offender** do to **you**? (Check all that apply.)

☐ none

☐ hug and/or kiss you

☐ fondle and/or massage your body

☐ rub his/her body against yours ("dry hump" or "dry fuck" you)

☐ masturbate you (give you a "hand job")

☐ put his/her finger in your ass ("finger fuck" you)

☐ perform oral sex on you (give you a "blow job")

☐ perform anal sex on you ("butt fuck" you)

☐ suck your ass ("rim" you)

☐ suck other parts of your body (for example, nipples, fingers, toes, etc.) If so, what parts?

☐ other sexual acts. Describe: _____

_____

_____

_____

13. Did the offender try to get you to ejaculate ("come off" or "shoot your load")?

☐ YES   ☐ NO   ☐ DON'T KNOW

14. Did he/she succeed?

☐ YES   ☐ NO   ☐ DON'T KNOW

15. Do you remember whether or not you had an orgasm (that is, the feeling of a sexual "high" or a "rush" of intense sexual pleasure)?

☐ YES, I did.   ☐ NO, I didn't.   ☐ I don't remember.

16. What type of sexual acts did the offender make **you** do?

☐ none

☐ hug and/or kiss him/her

☐ fondle and/or massage his/her body

- [ ] rub your body against his/hers ("dry hump" or "dry fuck" him/her)
- [ ] masturbate him/her (give him/her a "hand job")
- [ ] put your finger in his/her ass ("finger fuck" him/her)
- [ ] perform oral sex on him/her ("blow" him/"eat" her; "go down" on him/her)
- [ ] perform anal sex on him/her ("butt fuck" him/her)
- [ ] suck his/her ass ("rim" him/her)
- [ ] suck other parts of his/her body (for example, nipples, fingers, toes, etc.) If so, what parts?

_____

- [ ] masturbate yourself while he/she watched
- [ ] perform sex acts with another person while he/she watched. If so, what type of acts?
- [ ] other sexual acts. Describe: _____

_____

_____

_____

17. Describe how you felt at the time this happened in regard to the following:

a) Did you find this experience in any way *sexually pleasurable*?

☐ NO, not at all.
☐ YES, somewhat.
☐ YES, very much.
☐ Don't know.

b) Did you find this experience in any way *interesting*?

☐ NO, not at all.
☐ YES, somewhat.
☐ YES, very much.
☐ Don't know.

c) Did you find this experience in any way *exciting*?

☐ NO, not at all.
☐ YES, somewhat.
☐ YES, very much.
☐ Don't know.

d) Did you find this experience in any way *confusing*?

☐ NO, not at all.
☐ YES, somewhat.

☐ YES, very much.
☐ Don't know.

e) Did you find this experience in any way *frightening*?

☐ NO, not at all.
☐ YES, somewhat.
☐ YES, very much.
☐ Don't know.

f) Did you feel *depressed* about this happening?

☐ NO, not at all.
☐ YES, somewhat.
☐ YES, very much.
☐ Don't know.

g) Did you feel *upset* about this happening?

☐ NO, not at all.
☐ YES, somewhat.
☐ YES, very much.
☐ Don't know.

h) Did you feel *guilty* about this happening?

- ☐ NO, not at all.
- ☐ YES, somewhat.
- ☐ YES, very much.
- ☐ Don't know.

i) Did you feel this experience to be in any way *disgusting?*

- ☐ NO, not at all.
- ☐ YES, somewhat.
- ☐ YES, very much.
- ☐ Don't know.

j) Did you feel *angry* about this happening?

- ☐ NO, not at all.
- ☐ YES, somewhat.
- ☐ YES, very much.
- ☐ Don't know.

k) Did you feel *helpless?*

- ☐ NO, not at all.
- ☐ YES, somewhat.
- ☐ YES, very much.
- ☐ Don't know.

1) Were there any *other* feelings you had at the time in regard to this incident? If so, what were they? _____

_____

_____

18. What was the most troubling part of this experience for you? _____

_____

_____

19. Was there anything you liked or enjoyed about this experience at the time or anything you got out of it?

☐ YES   ☐ NO   ☐ DON'T KNOW

If *YES*, what was that? _____

_____

_____

20. Did you tell anybody about this at the time?

☐ YES　　☐ NO

[If NO, skip to question 21.]

Please answer the following:

a) Whom did you tell? _____

b) What were your reasons for telling? That is, what did you want to happen or what did you expect this person to do? _____

_____

_____

_____

c) How did the person you told react? What did they do? _____

_____

_____

_____

d) Was this person's response mostly:

☐ HELPFUL = made things better for the most part.

☐ HARMFUL = made things worse for the most part.

☐ INEFFECTUAL = neither made things better nor worse.

21. When this happened, did anyone find out about it in some way without your telling?

☐ YES ☐ NO

[If NO, skip to question 22.]

a) Who found out? _____

b) How did they discover this? _____

_____

_____

c) What was their reaction? What did they do? _____

_____

_____

d) Was this person's response mostly:

☐ HELPFUL = made things better for the most part.

☐ HARMFUL = made things worse for the most part.

☐ INEFFECTUAL = neither made things better nor worse.

22. If *NO*, why didn't you tell anyone at the time? _____

_____

_____

23. How serious or significant an event was this in regard to its effect on your life? How would you rate it on a scale from 1 (*unimportant*) to 10 (*extremely serious*)? _____

_____

_____

24. How many other times has something like this happened to you in your life? _____

Part D: FORCE

1. Were you ever physically forced or intimidated into some type of unwanted sexual activity?

   ☐ YES   ☐ NO   ☐ DON'T KNOW

   [If your answer is NO or DON'T KNOW, skip to Part E.]

2. What means did the offender use to get you to submit to sexual acts against your will? (Check all that apply.)

   ☐ used his/her authority as an adult over you

   ☐ incapacitated you with alcohol/drugs (got you drunk/"stoned")

   ☐ used verbal threats

   ☐ outnumbered you (gang assault)

   ☐ intimidated you with a weapon

   ☐ used some type of restraints to tie you up

   ☐ physically overpowered you

   ☐ attacked and beat you up

☐ other. Describe: _____

_____

_____

_____

Describe the circumstances and explain what happened and how it happened. _____

_____

_____

_____

3. How old were you the first time something like this happened to you? (If you don't know for sure, what would you guess your age to have been?) _____

4. How old was the other person(s)? (If you don't know for sure, what would you guess his/her age to have been?) _____

5. What was the sex of the other person(s)?

☐ MALE   ☐ FEMALE   ☐ BOTH

6. What was the relationship of that person to you (for example, parent, relative, friend, acquaintance, babysitter, teacher, scout leader, neighbor, stranger, etc.)? _____

7. How long did this person's sexual involvement with you last? Over what period of time (days, weeks, months, years) did this sexual activity continue with him/her? _____

8. How many times would you guess this person had sex with you in all? _____

9. Was this experience disturbing or troublesome to you in any way?

   ☐ YES   ☐ NO

   If *YES*, explain: _____

   _____

   _____

A-18

10. What type of sexual acts did the **offender** do to **you**? (Check all that apply.)

☐ none

☐ hug and/or kiss you

☐ fondle and/or massage your body

☐ rub his/her body against yours ("dry hump" or "dry fuck" you)

☐ masturbate you (give you a "hand job")

☐ put his/her finger in your ass ("finger fuck" you)

☐ perform oral sex on you (give you a "blow job")

☐ perform anal sex on you ("butt fuck" you)

☐ suck your ass ("rim" you)

☐ suck other parts of your body (for example, nipples, fingers, toes, etc.) If so, what parts? _____

☐ other sexual acts. Describe: _____
_____
_____
_____

11. Did the offender try to get you to ejaculate ("come off" or "shoot your load")?

☐ YES   ☐ NO   ☐ DON'T KNOW

12. Did he/she succeed?

☐ YES   ☐ NO   ☐ DON'T KNOW

13. Do you remember whether or not you had an orgasm (that is, the feeling of a sexual "high" or a "rush" of intense sexual pleasure)?

☐ YES, I did.   ☐ NO, I didn't.   ☐ I don't remember.

14. What type of sexual acts did the offender make **you** do?

☐ none

☐ hug and/or kiss him/her

☐ fondle and/or massage his/her body

☐ rub your body against his/hers ("dry hump" or "dry fuck" him/her)

☐ masturbate him/her (give him/her a "hand job")

☐ put your finger in his/her ass ("finger fuck" him/her)

☐ perform oral sex on him/her ("blow" him/"eat" her; "go down" on him/her)

☐ perform anal sex on him/her ("butt fuck" him/her)

A-19

☐ suck his/her ass ("rim" him/her)

☐ suck other parts of his/her body (for example, nipples, fingers, toes, etc.) If so, what parts? _____

_____

_____

☐ masturbate yourself while he/she watched

☐ perform sex acts with another person while he/she watched. If so, what type of acts? _____

_____

_____

☐ other sexual acts. Describe: _____

_____

_____

_____

15. Describe how you felt at the time this happened in regard to the following:

a) Did you find this experience in any way *sexually pleasurable?*

    ☐ NO, not at all.

☐ YES, somewhat.
☐ YES, very much.
☐ Don't know.

b) Did you find this experience in any way *interesting*?

☐ NO, not at all.
☐ YES, somewhat.
☐ YES, very much.
☐ Don't know.

c) Did you find this experience in any way *exciting*?

☐ NO, not at all.
☐ YES, somewhat.
☐ YES, very much.
☐ Don't know.

d) Did you find this experience in any way *confusing*?

☐ NO, not at all.
☐ YES, somewhat.
☐ YES, very much.
☐ Don't know.

e) Did you find this experience in any way *frightening*?

☐ NO, not at all.
☐ YES, somewhat.
☐ YES, very much.
☐ Don't know.

f) Did you feel *depressed* about this happening?

☐ NO, not at all.
☐ YES, somewhat.
☐ YES, very much.
☐ Don't know.

g) Did you feel *upset* about this happening?

☐ NO, not at all.
☐ YES, somewhat.
☐ YES, very much.
☐ Don't know.

h) Did you feel *guilty* about this happening?

☐ NO, not at all.
☐ YES, somewhat.
☐ YES, very much.
☐ Don't know.

i) Did you feel this experience to be in any way *disgusting*?

☐ NO, not at all.
☐ YES, somewhat.
☐ YES, very much.
☐ Don't know.

j) Did you feel *angry* about this happening?

☐ NO, not at all.
☐ YES, somewhat.
☐ YES, very much.
☐ Don't know.

k) Did you feel *helpless*?

☐ NO, not at all.
☐ YES, somewhat.
☐ YES, very much.
☐ Don't know.

l) Were there any other feelings you had at the time in regard to this incident?
    If so, what were they? _____

    _____

    _____

16. What was the most troubling part of this experience for you? _____

_____

_____

_____

17. Was there anything you liked or enjoyed about this experience at the time or anything you got out of it?

☐ YES ☐ NO ☐ DON'T KNOW

If *YES*, what was that? _____

_____

_____

18. Did you tell anybody about this at the time?

☐ YES ☐ NO

[If NO, skip to question 19.]

Please answer the following:

a) Whom did you tell? _____

b) What were your reasons for telling? That is, what did you want to happen or what did you expect this person to do? _____

_____

_____

_____

c) How did the person you told react? What did they do? _____

_____

_____

_____

d) Was this person's response mostly:

☐ HELPFUL = made things better for the most part.

☐ HARMFUL = made things worse for the most part.

☐ INEFFECTUAL = neither made things better nor worse.

A-22

19. When this happened, did anyone find out about it in some way without your telling?

☐ YES   ☐ NO

[If NO, skip to question 20.]

Please answer the following:

a) Who found out? _____

b) How did they discover this? _____
_____
_____

c) What was their reaction? What did they do? _____
_____
_____

d) Was this person's response mostly:

☐ HELPFUL = made things better for the most part.

☐ HARMFUL = made things worse for the most part.

☐ INEFFECTUAL = neither made things better nor worse.

20. If *NO*, why didn't you tell anyone at the time? _____

_____

_____

21. How serious or significant an event was this in regard to its effect on your life? How would you rate it on a scale from 1 (*unimportant*) to 10 (*extremely serious*)? _____

22. How many other times has something like this happened to you in your life? _____

Part E: OTHER SEXUAL TRAUMA

1. Were you ever exposed to any activities or behaviors of an intimate nature on the part of an older person which were personally upsetting or disturbing to you (such as sleeping with you, bathing you at an advanced age, or undressing in front of you)?

    ☐ YES   ☐ NO   ☐ DON'T KNOW

    [If NO or DON'T KNOW, skip to question 9.]

    Describe the incident and your feelings about it: _____

    _____

    _____

    _____

2. How old were you at the time? (If you don't know for sure, what would you guess your age to have been ?) _____

3. How old was the other person(s)? (If you don't know for sure, what would you guess his/her age to have been?) _____

4. What was the sex of the other person(s)?

☐ MALE   ☐ FEMALE   ☐ BOTH

5. What was the relationship of that person to you (for example, parent, relative, friend, acquaintance, babysitter, teacher, scout leader, neighbor, stranger, etc.)? _____

_____

6. How long did this go on? Over what period of time (once, days, weeks, months, years) did this continue? _____

_____

7. Was this experience disturbing or troublesome to you in any way?

☐ YES   ☐ NO

If *YES*, explain: _____

_____

_____

_____

A-24

8. How serious or significant an event was this in regard to its effect on your life? How would you rate it on a scale from 1 (*unimportant*) to 10 (*extremely serious*)? _____

9. Were you ever humiliated in a sexual fashion?

☐ YES ☐ NO ☐ DON'T KNOW

[If NO or DON'T KNOW, skip to question 17.]

Describe what happened: _____

_____

_____

9. How serious or significant an event was this in regard to its effect on your life? How would you rate it on a scale from 1 (*unimportant*) to 10 (*extremely serious*)? _____

10. How old were you at the time? (If you don't know for sure, what would you guess your age to have been? _____

11. How old was the other person(s)? (If you don't know for sure, what would you guess his/her age to have been?) _____

12. What was the sex of the other person(s)?

☐ MALE ☐ FEMALE ☐ BOTH

13. What was the relationship of that person to you (for example, parent, relative, friend, acquaintance, babysitter, teacher, scout leader, neighbor, stranger, etc.)? _____

14. How long did this go on? Over what period of time (once, days, weeks, months, years) did this continue? _____

15. Was this experience disturbing or troublesome to you in any way?

☐ YES ☐ NO

If *YES*, explain: _____

_____

_____

_____

16. How serious or significant an event was this in regard to its effect on your life? How would you rate it on a scale from 1 (*unimportant*) to 10 (*extremely serious*)? _____

17. Has anyone in your family or anyone close to you ever been a victim of sexual assault or sexual molestation?

☐ YES   ☐ NO, NOT THAT I KNOW OF

[If NO, skip to question 21.]

18. What *was* the relationship of this person to you? _____

19. How old were you when you found out about this? (If you don't know for sure, what would you guess your age to have been?) _____

20. Describe the incident as you know it. (Whom did it involve? What happened? How did it happen? Etc.) _____

_____

_____

_____

21. Were you ever involved in prostitution as a hustler?

☐ YES   ☐ NO   ☐ DON'T KNOW

[If NO or DON'T KNOW, skip to question 25.]

22. How did you get involved in or introduced to this activity? _____

_____

_____

_____

23. At what age did this begin? _____

24. How long did this go on? _____

25. Were you ever involved in pornography as a model (posing in the nude and/or engaging in sexual acts which were photographed, filmed, or videotaped)?

☐ YES   ☐ NO

[If NO, skip to question 27.]

26. How did you get involved in this enterprise? _____

_____

_____

27. Have you ever experienced any serious injuries to your sexual organs?

☐ YES   ☐ NO   ☐ DON'T KNOW

[If NO or DON'T KNOW, skip to question 28.]

a) At what age did this occur? (If you don't know for sure, what would you guess your age to have been?) _____

b) Was there any permanent harm or disability?

☐ YES   ☐ NO   ☐ DON'T KNOW

c) If *YES*, describe: _____

_____

_____

28. Have you been circumcised?

☐ YES   ☐ NO   ☐ DON'T KNOW

If *YES*, how old were you when this procedure was performed? _____

29. Have you ever had a venereal disease (syphilis, gonorrhea, etc.)?

☐ YES   ☐ NO   ☐ DON'T KNOW

a) If YES, at what age did this first occur? _____

b) About how many times has this happened to you? _____

30. Have you ever gotten into difficulty with the law because of your sexual behavior?

☐ YES   ☐ NO

[If NO, skip to question 31.]

a) How many times has this happened? _____

b) How old were you the first time this happened? (If you don't know for sure, what would you guess your age to have been?) _____

c) Explain what happened: _____

31. Are there any other sexual matters that concern you or additional information that you want to share?

☐ YES　　☐ NO

If *YES*, please explain: _____

Recommended Readings

Breer, William (1992) *Diagnosis and Treatment of the Young Male Victim of Sexual Abuse*. Springfield, IL: Charles C. Thomas Publishers Ltd.

Camino, Lisa (1999) *Treating Sexually Abused Boys: A Guide for Therapists and Counselors*. San Francisco, CA: Jossey-Bass.

Estrada, Hank (1994) *Recovery for Male Victims of Child Sexual Abuse*. Truth or Consequences, NM: Red Rabbit Press.

Etherington, Kim (2000) *Narrative Approaches to Working with Adult Male Survivors of Sexual Abuse: The Clients', the Counselors' and the Researchers' Stories*. University of Bristol, UK: Jessica Kingsley Publishers.

Friedrich, William N. (1995) *Psychotherapy with Sexually Abused Boys: An Integrated Approach* (Interpersonal Violence, the Practice Series, 12). Thousand Oaks, CA: Sage Publications.

Gartner, Richard B. (1999) *Betrayed as Boys: Psychodynamic Treatment of Sexually Abused Boys.* New York, NY: Guilford Publications.

Groth, A. Nicholas, and Birnbaum, H. J. (1979) *Men Who Rape: The Psychology of the Offender.* Cambridge, MA: Perseus Publishing.

Hunter, Mic (1990) *Abused Boys: The Neglected Victims of Sexual Abuse.* New York, NY: Fawcett Columbine.

Isensee, Rik (1997) *Reclaiming Your Life: The Gay Man's Guide to Love, Self-Acceptance, and Trust.* Los Angeles, CA: Alyson Publications.

King, Neal (1995) *Speaking Our Truth: Voices of Courage and Healing for Male Survivors of Childhood Sexual Abuse.* New York, NY: HarperCollins.

Lew, Mike (1988) *Victims No Longer: Men Recovering from Incest and Other Sexual Child Abuse.* New York, NY: Harper & Row.

Lew, Mike, and Hoffman, Richard (2000) *Leaping Upon the Mountains: Men Proclaiming Victory Over Sexual Child Abuse.* Berkeley, CA: North Atlantic Books.

Porter, Eugene (1986) *Treating the Young Male Victim of Sexual Assault.* Syracuse, NY: Safer Society Press.

Sanders, Timothy L. (1991) *Male Survivors: 12-Step Recovery Program for Survivors of Childhood Sexual Abuse.* Freedom, CA: Crossing Press.

Scarce, Michael (1997) *Male on Male Rape: The Hidden Toll of Stigma and Shame.* New York, NY: Insight Books/Plenum.

Tobin, Rod (1999) *Alone and Forgotten: The Sexually Abused Man.* Carp, Ontario, Canada: Creative Bound, Inc.

INTERNET RESOURCE

MaleSurvivor
(formerly the National Organization on Male Sexual Victimization—NOMSV)
5505 Connecticut Avenue, NW, Suite 103
Washington, DC 20015-2601

800-738-4181

Website: www.malesurvivor.org

About the Authors

John M. Preble, M.S.W. received his master's degree in social work from Fresno State University, California. He is licensed in the state of California as a clinical social worker and as a marriage and family therapist. His experience as a clinician includes working with abused children and their families, adult survivors of abuse, male victims of sexual abuse, and adolescent and adult sex offenders. He has run sexual abuse survivor groups for adult males, adolescents, and latency age boys as well as groups for the partners of adult survivors of sexual abuse. He has worked with victims and offenders in various settings including private nonprofit settings, a residential group home, and private practice. He was coordinator of the early childhood program for severely emotionally disturbed children at Child Guidance Center in Fullerton, California. He was a guest lecturer for Forensic Mental Health Associates and has presented on various aspects of child abuse at numerous professional workshops and conferences throughout southern California. He has served as a case consultant to community agencies and individual clinicians throughout southern California on clinical issues related to child abuse and adolescent sex offenders. His is the author of *The Ex-Offender's Guide To Survival* (Inside Out Press, 1981). Currently Mr. Preble is a full-time faculty/liaison at California State University San Bernardino, Department of Social Work where he teaches under a child welfare training grant.

A. Nicholas Groth, Ph.D. received his doctorate in clinical psychology from Boston University. He specialized in the area of sexual abuse and worked with both victims and offenders in a variety of institutional and community-based settings: He was Director of Psychological Services at the Center for the Diagnosis and Treatment of Sexually Dangerous Persons at the Massachusetts Correctional Institution in Bridgewater; Clinical Director at the Whiting Forensic Institute in Middleton, Connecticut; Director of the Forensic Mental Health Department at the Harrington Memorial Hospital Mental Health Clinic in Southbridge, Massachusetts; and Founder and Director of the Sex Offender Program of the Mental Hygiene Unit at the Connecticut Correctional Institution in Somers. He served as Consultant and Instructor to the Institute for Child Sexual Abuse Intervention at St. Joseph College in West Hartford, Connecticut, and on the Advisory Board for the National Center for the Prevention and Control of Rape, and the National Center on Child Abuse and Neglect in Washington, DC. In 1981 he established Forensic Mental Health Associates which provided nationwide education, consultation, and training in regard to sexual assault. Dr. Groth is the author of *Anatomical Drawings for Use in the Investigation and Intervention of Child Sexual Abuse* (F.M.H.A., 1990) and, together with H. Jean Birnbaum, of *Men Who Rape: The Psychology of the Offender* (Perseus Publishing, 1979); he is also the co-author of *Sexual Assault of Children and Adolescents* (Lexington Books, 1978). In addition, he has written numerous book chapters and journal articles on sexual assault and his writings have been translated into Swedish, Italian, French, and German. Dr. Groth is the recipient of the Stephen Schafer Award for Outstanding Research for the National Organization for Victim Assistance. He has lectured both nationally and internationally and has appeared on the *Today* show, *Good Morning America, 20/20*, the *Donahue* show, *Oprah,* and the *Montel Williams* show. He was also technical advisor for the ABC-TV movie *The Face of Rage* (1983), which was based on his work with convicted sex offenders and victims of sexual assault. Dr. Groth is now retired and resides in Orlando, Florida.

About the Sidran Institute

The **Sidran Institute, a leader in traumatic stress education and advocacy,** is a nationally focused nonprofit organization devoted to helping people who have experienced traumatic life events. Our education and advocacy promotes greater understanding of:

- The early recognition and treatment of trauma-related stress in children;

- The understanding of trauma and its long-term effect on adults;

- The strategies leading to greatest success in self-help recovery for trauma survivors;

- The clinical methods and practices leading to greatest success in aiding trauma victims;

- The development of public policy initiatives that are responsive to the needs of adult and child survivors of traumatic events.

To further this mission, Sidran operates the following programs:

The Sidran Press publishes books and educational materials on traumatic stress and dissociative conditions. A recently published example is *Growing Beyond Survival: A Self-Help Toolkit for Managing Traumatic Stress,* by Elizabeth Vermilyea. This innovative workbook provides skill-building tools to empower survivors to take control of their trauma symptoms.

Some of our other titles include *Risking Connection: A Training Curriculum for Working with Survivors of Childhood Abuse* (a curriculum for mental health professionals and paraprofessionals), *Managing Traumatic Stress Through Art* (an interactive workbook to promote healing), and *Understanding the Effects of Traumatic Stress* (a manual for community agencies.)

The Sidran Bookshelf on Trauma and Dissociation is an annotated mail order and web catalog of the best in clinical, educational, and survivor-supportive literature on post-traumatic stress, dissociative conditions, and related topics.

The Sidran Resource Center—drawing from Sidran's extensive database and library—provides resources and referrals at no cost to callers from around the English-speaking world. The referral database includes: trauma-experienced therapists, traumatic stress organizations, educational books and materials, conferences, trainings, and treatment facilities.

Sidran Education and Training Services provide conference speakers, pre-programmed and custom workshops, consultation, and technical assistance on all aspects of traumatic stress including:

- **Agency Training** on trauma-related topics, such as Trauma Symptom Management, Assessment and Treatment Planning, Borderline Personality Disorder, and others. We will be glad to customize presentations for the specific needs of your agency.

- **Survivor Education** programming including how to start and maintain effective peer support groups, community networking for trauma support, successful selection of therapists, coping skills, and healing skills.

- **Public Education** workshops on understanding PTSD and the psychological outcomes of severe childhood trauma for a variety of audiences: adult survivors, partners, and supporters; caregivers of abused children; and nonclinical professionals (such as teachers, social services personnel, clergy, etc.).

For more information on any of these programs and projects, please contact us:

The Sidran Institute
Traumatic Stress Education and Advocacy
200 East Joppa Road, Suite 207, Baltimore, MD 21286

Phone: 410-825-8888 • Fax: 410-337-0747
E-mail: help@sidran.org • Website: www.sidran.org